# TEMPTATION

## Your Destiny Signal

## CURTIS BRACY

### THEWARFAREPREACHER

Consulted By:

a Division of Carr Corp Enterprises, LLC
Ashericarr.com

# CONTENTS

# FOREWORD

One of the greatest challenges of the Apostolics today is the ability to overcome temptation. Temptation is defined as the desire to do something, especially something wrong or unwise. According to the scriptures, each of us battles temptation, but there is a way to overcome and be victorious. Many youth and elders alike are failing, due to the lack of Bible strategies to overcome such intense battling for enduring years. Elder Bracy provides, in this unique book, an effective means of approaching temptations by addressing the issue at hand as well as investigating the source from which many of these battles come. Elder Bracy has provided a level of transparency that makes it comfortable to any struggling saint assuring them that they are not alone. Each chapter provides a new wealth of information that every saint will need to approach these challenges with confidence. It is certain that we may have all the knowledge of our battles but having knowledge without tools and strategies is not enough. All tools are not effective for everyone. We all have our own battles; therefore, we must have our own tools to help assist in the fight against temptation. If you have been wounded and scarred by Satan or your flesh is your battle to overcome, this book is what you need to discover, recover, and overcome!

In Jesus' Name
Apostle C.A. Cowart
DD, DRS, Bachelor of Legal Studies

# DEDICATION

This book is dedicated to the Memory of my Grandmother, Pastor, and Presiding Elder Anna Cooper. You have instilled confidence in me that hell cannot steal. That confidence is in Christ Jesus.

To my mother, Prophet Loria Bracy, for letting me know to never stop at enough.

To my best friend, the love of my life, and gorgeous wife: the lovely Lady Shadae Bracy.

To my Father in the gospel and Pastor, Bishop Mark E. Parrott, Sr. for being the "Truth Teller."

To the Lighthouse Temple Church of the Church Our LORD Jesus Christ of the Apostolic Faith Inc. (COOLJC). I love you all tremendously.

Malcolm Smiley, the photographer. Thank you for all your hard work and patience, my bro. You rock bro.

To Deacon Asher Carr. Brother, you are the right man for the job. Thank you for helping bring my vision to life.

# CONTENT WARNING

This book contains the following sensitive topics:

Abuse, neglect & abandonment

Anxiety disorders & anxiety attacks

Body shaming

Cheating

Depression

Drug abuse

Mental illness

Panic attacks

Rape

Sexual abuse

Verbal abuse

Some topics may bring up thoughts and emotions that can be overwhelming and should be tackled under the guidance of mental health or other support professionals.

# INTRODUCTION

It's a matter of life and death. It's what separates the boys from the men. It can be something we conquer or something that conquers us. Yes, it's temptation. If we think we can outlive it, think again. If we think we can out-preach it, go back to Bible study. If we think marriage will cure porn addictions, we might need more than sex rehab. If you think changing your identity and moving to another state is the only way to erase your past, unpack your luggage and save your gas money.

This one word is deadly, but the sound of it is appealing to many of us. An R&B group was named after it. A movie was produced by Tyler Perry about the downside of it. Many say that sex is overrated, but what is sex without the foreplay of temptation? What good is all work without play? What good is a relationship without some flirting on the side?

What is it about temptation that pulls us in and makes us risk it all? Temptation gives us a distraction from the highs and lows of life. Temptation will make us feel wanted, and desirable, and appears to take the load off. The instant gratification we get gives us something to think about during the long hours at work. The fast money we make during the wee hours of the night helps us to cope with the depression and anxiety of living on minimum wage.

Temptation is what our parents warned us about, but we did not listen. We were young and knew everything, so we decided that we were stronger than the temptation that was designed to destroy us. You saw your brother go through drug addiction, but you thought you were an exception to the rule. Your girlfriends warned you to leave that married man alone, but you just knew that you had the goods to make him leave his wife. Your mother told you to find a woman that loves you for you, but you wanted the girl who did not want to be wanted.

Nevertheless, we cannot blame all this on temptation. You see, temptation alone is harmless, useless, and won't hurt a fly. Temptation needs you. Read that again. Temptation needs you. It is nothing at all without your help. Temptation needs our cravings and insecurities, childhood wounds, deep dark secrets, loss, and loneliness to do some real damage. Although the temptation is nothing without you, it wants you to think you're nothing without it.

Temptation is a backstabbing self-esteem booster. It makes the insecure think too highly of themselves for the moment but will leave them with their head in their hands when it's all said and done. Temptation makes the lonely wife feel desirable again but sends her emotions on an emotional roller coaster ride when the secret lover ghosted her. Temptation will make you feel like you're on top of the world while we are cheating the IRS. Nevertheless, it will have us feel crazy when the law catches up with us.

It is the insecurities of temptation that do real damage. It is the relentless thought that if we do not give in to it, we won't be complete and satisfied. Temptation is out to make us think we are less than who Jesus Christ already created us to be. Temptation will have us settling for moments of instant gratification rather than trusting in the LORD Jesus Christ for the long-term plan. Yes, temptation will embarrass the celebrity, take the wealth of the richest mind, and destroy a couple that was going through a bad season in the right relationship.

However, we have reduced temptation to sex, lust, and lies. However, temptation is after more than our need for arousal, stimulation, or an orgasm. Temptation wants to do more than show us a good time and take us for a night out into the wild. Temptation is after the soul. It's after the will to serve God. It's after our peace of mind. More importantly, temptation is after our destiny. Temptation is the confirmation that the LORD Jesus Christ has a purpose in your life.

When many of us are discouraged about how long the process is to get what we prayed for, reach our goals, and enjoy the "good life," we may call a trusted friend, pray harder, or some have gone as far as consulting fortune tellers. Many of us have not realized that the greatest signal to our destiny has been in our lives the whole time. That is temptation. If we can endure it, we will see our God-ordained destiny unfold.

I will use the life of Joseph from the book of Genesis, to show us the many ways that temptation presents itself. So as you turn the page, you will delve into the many temptations that you or someone you are concerned about are secretly battling.

# The Temptation to Shut Down

"Your Secrets are Safe with Me. I'll be like
the Pages in Your Diary." – Alicia Keys

There are some people we wish and hope to never run into again. There are some people that we have changed our phone numbers to avoid. There are some people that we have relocated to get away from. They have hurt us so badly, left us so vulnerable, and sent us into an abyss of chronic anxiety to the degree to which, we wouldn't even go to their funeral to say our final goodbyes.

These are not our past employers, old childhood friends, or even an ex-lover. These are family members. Some of our parents prepared us to go out into "the real world." They warned us about how cold the real world can be. They explained to us how shady the Judas in our own lives can be. However, they did not warn or prepare us that sometimes that cold world is right in the same house that we grew up in that they wanted us to call home. Jesus Christ put it this way:

> *"Well-meaning family members can be your worst enemies" (Matthew 10:36, MSG)*

This is what Joseph had to learn the hard way. The family way.

> *"Joseph could stand it no longer. There were many people in the room, and he said to his attendants, "Out, all of you!" So he was alone with his brothers when he told them who he was. Then he broke down and wept. He wept so loudly the Egyptians could hear him, and word of it quickly carried to Pharaoh's palace. "I am Joseph!" he said to his brothers. "Is my father still alive?" But his brothers were speechless! They were stunned to realize that Joseph was standing there in front of them. "Please, come closer," he said to them. So they came closer. And he said again, "I am Joseph, your brother, whom you sold into slavery in Egypt" (Genesis 45:1-4, NLT).*

After thirteen years of not seeing his brothers, they did not recognize him. They did not even think he was alive. They thought that the enemies they sold him to had finished him off. **Little did they understand that you can't finish off who Jesus Christ is not finished with.** Since they last saw Joseph, he was

> **Little did they understand that you can't finish off who Jesus Christ is not finished with.**

stripped of his coat of many colors, despised by his brothers, and hated. They are now in a famine, in need of food, and little did they know that they would need the same brother who they made an outcast. **God has a way of making us run into people we planned on avoiding forever.**

## I Was Going to Call You

You remember that phrase, don't you? We often bumped into people who went MIA (missing in action) on us, or have called them because they were not returning our call only to hear them say, "I was going to call you." Sometimes those words are hiding the passive-aggressiveness of those who don't want to have anything else to do with us and are too cowardly to tell us or want us to figure out what is going on and read their mind.

Joseph was the total opposite. He wanted to reunite with his brothers, but he still is affected by what they did to him. Although their betrayal did not affect his character; it affected his idea of family. Joseph was family oriented. He believed he could tell his family everything. However, families are not exempt from thoughts and feelings of jealousy, rage, resentment, and hatred. We know that a family that prays together stays together. However, little did Joseph realize that families that communicate together, don't always stay together. As Kevin Hart would say, "You gonna learn today."

## CAN I TELL YOU SOMETHING?

*"One night Joseph had a dream, and when he told his brothers about it, they hated him more than ever. "Listen to this dream," he said. "We were out in the field, tying up bundles of grain. Suddenly my bundle stood up, and your bundles all gathered around and bowed low before mine!" His brothers responded, "So you think you will be our king, do you? Do you actually think you will reign over us?" And they hated him all the more because of his dreams and the way he talked about them" (Genesis 37:5-8, NLT).*

After reading the above passage, you might have said to yourself, "why are they tripping; it was just a dream?" Nevertheless, I have come to find out that it is the jealousy of those close to us that reveals what Jesus Christ placed in our spirits, hearts, and mind are more than just dreams. When God wants to confirm the dreams in our spirit that is about to be a reality in our lives, it is often confirmed by the envy of our loved ones. Sad? Yes. True? Absolutely!

Joseph is in a family that he can eat with, work with, and be with. He just can't talk about his dreams with them. He opens up to them about the dream that includes them, but they become jealous and instantaneously hateful towards him over what God has put in his heart. **Hear me when I say, if some of your** family has not fought against the dream that Christ has given you, it is not a Jesus dream.

**family has not fought against the dream that Christ has given you, it is not a Jesus dream.**

## Family Feud

Actor Steve Harvey does a great job of making us laugh as the host of *Family Feud.* Some of us have gotten a kick out of watching this show, laughing and trying to answer the questions just as quickly as the contestants on the show. However, family feuds in real life are not fun and games.

Family feuds in real life will create years of silent treatment, long-term resentment, deceitful gossip, and division as we have never seen. Many think families only divide at weddings, funerals, or when the matriarch of the family goes on to be with the LORD Jesus. If you want to see a real family feud, let Jesus give you a dream.

Joseph never thought that his life would have taken the turn that it took for telling his parents and brothers about his dream. Joseph learned real fast that everything in our heads can't be shared with everyone, even the people that we love. What do you do when there is more love in the streets than in your house? What do you do when you're more respected in the workplace than you are at home? Joseph is not the typical rebellious, seventeen-year-old. Joseph is obedient to his parents, and loving to his brothers, but he was different from everyone in the house.

Sometimes, it hurts to be unique when all we want is to be understood by those we love. He was hated because of his dreams. They were envious of him because of his identity and the demonstrated love of the father for him. Often the people who love create enemies for us. Joseph did not ask to be favored, but God has other plans.

## I Wasn't Always Like This

I grew up in a family of preachers. It was in our blood. My grandmother was a preacher. My uncles and aunts were preachers. Some of my cousins are preachers. It runs in the family. How- ever, I knew Jesus Christ gave me a different sound for the generation he wanted me to reach. I was not always understood. At those moments, I had to trust in the LORD Jesus who gave me the gift. There were times when it was frustrating trying to explain to the preachers in my family what the LORD told me to say or do because it didn't match or line up with their way of saying or doing things.

Joseph was not always aware of his God-given dreams. However, he was always his father's favorite. This tempted his brothers to hate him. Once their father, Jacob, gave Joseph a coat of many colors- it was on and popping. When we feel our parents favor one child over the other, it will often tempt us to be something we are not to win their approval. Others will be tempted to become bitter and resentful towards the favored one. However, the coat did not cause as much jealousy as the dream.

## A Lesson on the Jealousy of Temptation

How do you talk and share your dreams with someone jealous of you? **Those who are jealous of us hold back their real thoughts when we are trying to communicate with**

**them. A jealous individual's presence is not a threat; it's their private thoughts.** How can we be family, and you're secretly plotting against me? How can we be close, and you're only playing me close to know my secrets, learn how I do what I do, and sabotage my future? How can your best friend help you pick out your wedding dress and sleep with your spouse?

> Those who are jealous of us hold back their real thoughts when we are trying to communicate with them. A jealous individual's presence is not a threat; it's their private thoughts.

Jealousy is often out of the hearts of people who we love most and thought were our confidants and not our opponents. Often strangers can become our biggest fans before friends and family. However, what makes jealous people jealous is that they don't know or believe in what Jesus Christ the LORD has called them to do so. They are so fixated on what the person they are jealous of is doing that they minimize the call of Christ on their life.

If you want to know what real praise is. It's when you are content with who you are in Jesus Christ. When we stop comparing ourselves to others who we deem better looking, smarter, classier, or successful, our unique identity will be a praise to God! Value who you are in him. Don't just praise God for who HE is; praise Jesus Christ for who you are in. *"In him we live and move and exist"* (Acts 17:28, NLT).

## I THOUGHT I COULD COME TO YOU

Once Joseph revealed his dream of his brothers bowing down to him, it forever changed how they looked at him. **Many**

**of us are scared and feel wounded today because we have been looked at differently by the people who we shared our dreams with.** Many children had to grow up quickly because they were shot down for sharing their dreams with parents, siblings, or relatives who were envious of their dreams.

> Many of us are scared and feel wounded today because we have been looked at differently by the people who we shared our dreams with.

At 17, Joseph learned not to trust everyone he talked to. He learned that it's not always safe to share a thought with those who secretly envy you. Joseph had to face the temptation of opening up again by the time he saw his brothers again. When they saw their brother again, those tables had turned. He is now in a place of power. Pharaoh has given him a position that would make the fellas envy him and the woman chases after him. However, success does not make us open up, especially after we learned the hard way.

## WHEN I SAID SOMETHING, NO ONE BELIEVED ME

There are people right now that has silenced themselves from the ones that love them because of the people they loved that did not believe them. It hurts to be loved but not believed. It's one thing if you give someone reason to doubt you based on multiple mistakes from the past. However, in Joseph's case, he did nothing wrong. He is dealing with the temptation of shutting down. Yes, not being believed will make us not want to say anything else.

I do, however, want to take a minute and talk to all of you who are quiet because you have allowed guilt to hold you. Hear me when I tell you, the people whose opinions you are afraid of are sitting on the past themselves. I promised the LORD Jesus Christ that I would never allow what people know or think they know about me to stop me from being bold, confident, and assertive with the assignment that he has given me. As Bishop T. D. Jakes, once stated, "Whatever you did that made them hate you, do it some more." **Sometimes it is not what you did wrong that makes them hate you. It's the audacity to finally do right with your head up and it makes the hair on their neck stand up.**

## BODY LANGUAGE DON'T LIE

When I speak of the temptation to shut down, I am speaking more of shutting down by not talking. Some shut down by refusing to be intimate. Many who are comfortable with sex aren't comfortable with intimacy. **You have to know who you are being intimate with someone else. However, you** can be who you want to be when there are no strings attached in the bedroom.

**can be who you want to be when there are no strings attached in the bedroom.**

Many of us have shut down in our body language with a closed-off demeanor. We are not approachable. We are constantly in protective mode. We know what it's like to open up to people, and they use it against us, minimize our feelings, or have us feeling embarrassed for being honest. Many of us are as cuddly as a teddy bear but have the demeanor of a pit bull only out of the fear of being vulnerable.

You may be saying, "Give me a break man! Do you want me to just go around opening up to total strangers?" Absolutely not. I do, however, want you to stop opening up to people who just want to sleep with you and leave you. I do want you to stop opening up to people who have already proven that they are snakes. I want you to stop opening up to your work husband about what your real husband is not doing. Sometimes, when we have been betrayed for opening up to the people we love, we find ourselves telling the right things to the wrong people.

## MOVING IN SILENCE

You can go for years with an untold story, an unconfessed secret, or unconfronted pain on the inside of you. We do it every day. It had been thirteen years since Joseph has seen his brothers, and they don't know he was still affected by what they did to him. They don't even know that he is alive. Joseph does not have a therapist, psychologist, or psychiatrist that he could go to. Joseph does what many of us have been conditioned to do; move in silence. Here are some reasons why we move in silence:

- Guilt

When people have placed us on a pedestal, we fear letting them down, so we keep our sins and mistakes to ourselves. However, the guilt becomes overwhelming. So we remain married with this guilt; buy houses with this guilt; help other people address their guilt; and continue to suffer in silence. Guilt won't stop us from being successful, but it will keep us from enjoying it.

- Not Knowing How They Will React

A woman once told me, "It's hard to live with someone you're scared of." Recording artist, Lupe Fiasco once said, "I think the silence is worse than all the violence. Fear is such a weak emotion, that's why I despise it. We are scared of almost everything, afraid to even tell the truth. So scared of what you think of me I'm even scared of telling the truth." Many of us are afraid to lose people by letting them know how we feel inside, which creates a special kind of loneliness.

We make love with people we are afraid to confess to, and will stay in houses with people we tell everything to except our secrets. We wonder how they look at us, what they think of us, and if they will leave us or not. We wonder if we will be judged for sharing what really happened. Yes, they may yell, scream, and even curse. They are upset that we kept it from them. They may even ask, "Why didn't you come to me?"

- Unsupportive

Joseph did not get the reaction that he thought he would get. They did not support his dreams the way he expected them to. We are lying to ourselves if we say that we don't want to be celebrated. Everyone wants to be celebrated. God is not against us wanting to be celebrated. He just does not want us to be braggarts and pompous. He wants us to celebrate with him in mind and at the forefront. When we open our mouths to talk about our blessing and success, he wants us to give all the praise, honor, and glory to HIM alone. He doesn't even mind others celebrating us either, for the scripture says, "Let another man praise thee, not thine own mouth" (Proverbs 27:2, KJV).

God will often reduce our circle, and eliminate the people that we wanted the most support from to show us where our real help comes from. I have learned to trust who God sends into my life even if I am not used to them at first. **God will often sit us next to those who we are not comfortable with to teach us how to be comfortable with the unique parts of ourselves that we didn't know were inside of us.**

- Not Wanting to Hurt the Ones We Love

I never will forget watching the Maury show one day when a man confessed to his girl-friend that he is the father of her grandson. Yes! You read right. He slept with her daughter. He brought her on the show because he did not know how to tell her on his own. Our loved ones and the people in our circle deserve the truth. They should hear it from us before hearing it from someone else.

# Why Didn't You Say Something?

Guarded people don't open up as fast and easily as others do. Some have been hurt and learned to forgive, understanding that hurt is a part of life. Others have internalized the hurt so much that their feelings of worthiness have been shot that they have lost total hope in their future. **Many of us have kicked the right people out of our lives when they were only trying to help.**

> **Many of us have kicked the right people out of our lives when they were only trying to help.**

Many of us were asked after revealing painful secrets, and hurtful confessions, "Why didn't you say something sooner?" what they didn't realize is that we started talking to the wrong people about the right things. We might have shut down with them, but have opened up to some- one else. I once heard a story about a man who went off to war. He wrote his wife 365 letters. Guess who she slept with? She slept with the mailman. When her husband confronted her about it, she said, "The mailman was there."

We are social creatures and we need someone to talk to. Foxes go to their holes. Birds go to the nest. We go to each other. Joseph had no one that he could talk to in his father's house. At thirty, he was in the palace. He had success, wealth, a good boss, and enough money to take care of his brothers who just knew that Joseph was dead or alive in chains. They didn't trust the God that Joseph talked to.

And they needed him and didn't know they needed him. Be careful who you shut down on because you will never know if you need them to open up for you. There was a famine going on back in Joseph's hometown where his brothers were staying.

Joseph was now the COO (Chief Operating Officer) in Egypt. When his brothers showed up they did not recognize him. Oh yes, Joseph did not look like what he had been through.

## You Didn't Take Me Seriously

Joseph's brothers were freaked out. Scared to death to know that the man standing in front of them was the same brother they wanted to get rid of. Many have mistreated you that don't even realize that the next time they see you again, you will be in a place of blessing and power. When Joseph told them his dreams at 17, they didn't take them seriously; they only took the plot they had to kill him seriously.

The LORD Jesus spoke to me a few years ago and said to me that many who like me now will hate me later. Sadly, He was not referring to strangers. There were many close to me. Believe it or not, they were once celebrators. No one knows how to frustrate us like the ones who use to celebrate us. Their hatred for you will sound louder than their applause for you. However, **I had to learn quickly that sometimes people come, see people go, and keep going.**

## I Can't Talk Right Now

You've heard the saying, "You're a better man/woman than me" right? Joseph did not avoid speaking to his brothers about what happened. He confronted them from a healed place. **Many**

> **Many say some things are better left unsaid. However, I say to you that some things are better said from a healed place.**

**say some things are better left unsaid. However, I say to you that some things are better said from a healed place.** A healed place is a place of peace that can only come from the prince of peace. Let's be clear: Jesus Christ is our peace, according to Ephesians 2:14.

Have you been avoiding the conversation with the molester in your family, who you see at every family reunion but lack the courage to confront? Are you in a suppressed place that it hurts so bad to discuss it? Or, are you trying not to rock the boat and upset the family name? Haven't you noticed that what you aren't confronting is messing up your marriage, work production, and sanity, and even interfering with the time you spend with Jesus Christ in prayer? Please don't allow your pride to get the best of you. As Dr. Dharius Daniels, Pastor of Change Church says, "Pride is insecurity playing dress up."

## YOU TALK TOO MUCH

I wish Joseph did have a therapist to go to, but he didn't. I wish Joseph did have Dr. Phil to watch, but the tv wasn't invented in his day nor was the radio station. All Joseph had was his integrity and a walk with God. When we study the life of Joseph, we see how he keeps this family secret of betrayal to himself. He has made up his mind to no longer be the guy who "talks too much" anymore.

Many of us have had our secrets told that we shared in confidence, had our words diminished, and have had our

**However, in an endeavor to shut down about our pain, we have stopped talking about the Christ of our future. You, my friend, need to start talking.**

words twisted so much so that we have vowed to never say another word again. **However, in an endeavor to shut down about our pain, we have stopped talking about the Christ of our future. You, my friend, need to start talking.** Speaking of talking, the LORD Jesus is leading me to ask you when was the last time you prayed in the spirit? To pray in the Spirit is to pray under the power of the Holy Spirit's influence.

Hurt people must pray. Wounded hearts must pray. Bitter people must pray. Praying in tongues takes your prayer life to another dimension. Why? Satan cannot get in on the conversation.

The Bible made it clear that when we speak in tongues we speak directly to God (See 1 Corinthians chapter 14). The more we remain shut down, we will continuously be torn down mentally, physically, and emotionally. However, the word of God makes it clear that praying in the spirit builds us up (Jude 1:20).

Aren't you tired of remaining quiet to appease people who don't want you to rock the boat? Aren't you tired of holding onto things that are making you mentally and physically ill? Aren't you tired of lashing out about things that trigger you that you refuse to go to therapy and address? If you are not filled with the Holy Spirit, lift your hands right where you are and ask the LORD Jesus Christ to fill you with the HOLY GHOST. They that call on the name of the LORD shall be saved (Acts 2:21,38-39). His name is JESUS.

# I Can't Believe You're Still Talking About This

Yes, there can be people that are insensitive to what we have been through. We are the "Get Over It" culture. We want everything fast-paced, even our traumas. People who are insensitive to our past trauma aren't trying to be mean. Sometimes they came from families where everything was swept under the rug. Additionally, in most cases, they might have not dealt with their trauma. Consequently, hearing about ours is reminding them of theirs.

## Giving Closure to the Ones Whose Closure We Thought We Needed

His brother's never explained why they treated him that way- and God never explained why he gave Joseph those two dreams at seventeen which became a reality by the time he turned thirty. Furthermore, do you want to know something else? Joseph never asked his brothers for closure. Let us repeat what he said when he finally decides to reveal to his brothers who he was:

> *"Joseph could stand it no longer. There were many people in the room, and he said to his attendants, "Out, all of you!" So he was alone with his brothers when he told them who he was. Then he broke down and wept. He wept so loudly the Egyptians could hear him, and word of it quickly carried to Pharaoh's palace. "I am Joseph!" he said to his brothers. "Is*

*my father still alive?" But his brothers were speechless! They were stunned to realize that Joseph was standing there in front of them. "Please, come closer," he said to them. So they came closer. And he said again, "I am Joseph, your brother, whom you sold into slavery in Egypt. But don't be upset, and don't be angry with yourselves for selling me to this place. It was God who sent me here ahead of you to preserve your lives. This famine that has ravaged the land for two years will last five more years, and there will be neither plowing nor harvesting. God has sent me ahead of you to keep you and your families alive and to preserve many survivors. So it was God who sent me here, not you! And he is the one who made me an adviser to Pharaoh—the manager of his entire palace and the governor of all Egypt" (Genesis 45:1-8, NLT).*

Joseph was not worried about why they did what they did. He is just making sure they understand that it was more than an evil plot on their part. It was a divine setup on God's part. What his brothers meant for evil, God made it good (Genesis 50:20). **Many of us want closure from people who don't know that God was using them the whole time to get us to our predestined place.**

## LESSONS ON TEMPTATION: "HERE COMES THE DREAMER"

Temptation watches how you talk to yourself about yourself. When we put ourselves down, we are opening the door for the temptation to come into our lives at the most inconvenient times. The scriptures tell us what Joseph told his father and brothers about his dream. However, we have no information on what Joseph said to himself about his dreams. Maybe Joseph never had a conversation with himself about how his brothers would respond. Maybe Joseph never told himself, after his brother's first sarcastic responses, that his brothers are not happy for him.

They referred to Joseph as "the dreamer" (Genesis 37:19). They no longer remind each other that he is their brother. They have changed their dialogue about him. **Regardless of who changes their view of you, hold on to the vision that Jesus Christ gave you about you.** Joseph always held on to his identity despite what others said about him, even if they were family.

Temptation is after our identity. If satan can emotionally, verbally, or physically abuse us through the people that we love, he knows it can affect our view of who we are in Christ Jesus. Remember when satan came to tempt Jesus, he said, *"If you are the Son of God, tell these stones to become loaves of bread"* (*Matthew 4:3, NLT*). Jesus, however, being God in the flesh, knew how to respond to Satan's attack on his identity. Jesus responded by saying, *"No! The Scriptures say, 'People do not live by bread alone, but by every word that comes from the mouth of God'"* (Matthew 4:4, NLT).

When we give into the temptation to shut down because of the ones who shot down our dreams with their negative reactions, we will be subconsciously closed off to what came out of the mouth of God about us. To overcome the temptation to shut down, we must remember that God did not shut his mouth about what he said about us. We are who Christ says we are even when temptation is lurking in our direction.

## IF YOU DON'T SAY IT, I WILL

I often wonder how Joseph's life would have turned out if he would have kept quiet about the dreams that the LORD gave him. Maybe he would have never had his brothers plot against him. If Joseph had kept quiet, he probably would have never been placed in a pit. If Joseph would have kept his dreams to himself, he would have never been sold into slavery, and, ultimately, placed in jail.

However, **if Joseph kept quiet to avoid pain, he would have never tasted success.** Let me pause and ask you what you are trying to avoid by staying quiet. Are you trying to remain in the clique? Are you trying to keep your connection with people who you think have the power to take you to the top? Are you trying to avoid speaking what God put in your spirit because you don't want the family to treat you like an outcast? Need I remind you that "If God is for us, who can be against us" (Romans 8:31)?

Some of us are quiet because we don't want our secrets exposed. Are you living in a chronic state of anxiety, allowing yourself to be blackmailed? There's an old saying. "tell the truth, or someone else will tell it for you." Please don't continue to live in fear of being exposed for who you used to be. Even if you are in it now, God is calling you out of those secret sins. "Go, and sin no more" (John 8:11).

## You Have Unresolved Communication

Many of us aren't talking because we don't want to feel the pain and relive the memories all over again. Let me tell you something. You think therapy is expensive. Try to live with the secret of regrets, past issues, trauma never discussed secret drug addictions, and even secret affairs. It's not talking about it that makes it worse. We aren't just tempted to shut down on others, but we also shut down on ourselves. Furthermore, **if we aren't careful we will shut down on God without realizing it.**

> **if we aren't careful we will shut down on God without realizing it.**

You have to talk about it before it kills you. You have to talk about it before your kidney fails due to hypertension from the stress of keeping everything in. **You have to talk about it before you lose another relationship by acting out what you need to talk out.** For your information, this chapter is not about opening up when you are down. It is about the temptation of shutting down even though you are on your feet.

> **You have to talk about it before you lose another relationship by acting out what you need to talk out.**

This is the mistake we make thinking that we can succeed successfully with hidden pain in our hearts. This will get us into trouble every single time. Unaddressed pain will affect your marriage. Unaddressed secrets will create bigger ones and destroy trust. Haven't you noticed even in Hollywood, with fame and fortune, it doesn't fix the unresolved issues that Celebrities have? Success doesn't heal secrets, trauma, or unresolved pain. It will only expose what's been covered. Are you ready to step into the light?

## Opening Up to the Same People

Who hasn't made this mistake? We have all opened up to someone that we realized, later on, was not the one to vent or open up to. Consequently, we find ourselves frustrated, angry, discouraged, and sometimes feeling stupid that we opened up to another person that we thought we could trust. Joseph's family is the first group of people in scripture that we see him open up to.

Opening up to the family he thought he could trust almost cost him his life. However, God's plans for Joseph kept him alive. Sometimes, as preachers, we criticize Joseph for opening up and sharing his dreams. However, God never reprimanded him for doing so. God wants you to know that **just because they are jealous of the dream God gave you doesn't make you wrong for sharing.** I want to thank you for sharing your dream. Why? When your enemies see it come to fruition, they can say, "I remember when." And you'll be able to say it was the LORD's doing, and it's marvelous in your eyes (Mark 12:11).

## Just Hear Me Out

*"On the third day, Joseph spoke to them. "Do this and you'll live. I'm a God-fearing man. If you're as honest as you say you are, one of your brothers will stay here in jail while the rest of you take the food back to your hungry families. But you have to bring your youngest brother back to me, confirming the truth of your speech—and not one of you will die." They agreed. Then they started talking among themselves. "Now we're paying for what we did to our brother—we saw how terrified he was when he was begging us for mercy. We wouldn't listen to him and now we're the ones in trouble." Reuben broke in. "Didn't I tell you, 'Don't hurt the boy'? But no, you wouldn't listen. And now we're paying for his murder" (Genesis 42:18-22, MSG).*

It is true that some memories just don't go away. Marrying a good man doesn't always erase the verbal abuse of the bad one. The good words of the adopted mother do not erase the bad words of the blood mother. The truth of the matter is some things do go away. When Joseph saw his brothers again, he had to teach himself how to keep his composure because he could not hold back the tears. Yes, as tough as your exterior appears to look to others, some tears you can't stop from falling.

Joseph had pleaded with his brothers to treat him right. He didn't know the intensity of jealousy they

> **It's hard to communicate our love to those who hear us through the perception of their insecurities.**

had against him. He probably vowed to never talk about his dreams to them ever again while pleading to be free from their hateful plot. Nevertheless, they wouldn't hear him out. All they saw was how insecure his dreams were making them feel. **It's hard to communicate our love to those who hear us through the perception of their insecurities.**

## TIMING IS EVERYTHING

*"A fool uttereth all his mind: but a wise man keepeth it in till afterwards"* (Proverbs 29:11, KJV). When we have held things in for so long, they don't always come out right. Subsequently, by the time we get ready to open up, it comes out the wrong way. Joseph did not open up all at once. A fool and a wise man can feel all things at once, but a wise man knows that he can't share all at once, and he knows who not to share it with and he knows the respectful yet assertive way to communicate to express their feelings.

Joseph's brothers have a conscience that is eating away at them but they don't realize that the brother they ruled out would be the one to rule over them. They did realize that Joseph's steps were being ordered by God even if God had to use his enemies to do it. The clock was not against Joseph; it was working for him. Because Joseph was on God's clock, he had to under- stand that there is a time to speak, and a time to be silent.

# TESTIFY

Many of us have a chapter in our story that we don't read out loud. Some of us are afraid of how others will view us. Your story is more than a story. It's what the Bible calls a testimony. Someone needs to hear what Jesus Christ has brought us through. The trick of the enemy is to entice us to fabricate, modify, and alter our story to calm guilt, shame, and remorse. Don't just tell your testimony; tell the whole testimony. The Bible makes it clear that we overcome the devil by the blood of the lamb (LORD Jesus Christ, our Great God, and Savior) and the word of our testimony, according to Revelation 12:11.

Don't deny what Jesus Christ has brought you through. It's the parts we are afraid to talk about that God has brought us through the most. The devil would love for you not to tell your testimony of how Jesus Christ brought you through unemployment, healed you of past trauma, was there when everyone else walked away and wiped private tears from your eyes.

Why would the devil love you to be silent about your testimony? Well, the devil knows that if you tell your testimony, so many others will be set free. If even one person is changed by your testimony, heaven still rejoices over one sinner that repents than ninety-nine righteous, according to Luke 15:10. Tell your testimony. Go tell it on the mountain, over the hills, and everywhere. In fact, tell your molester, the rapist, the gang member who shot your loved one, and the sister that slept with your man that Jesus Christ is LORD and your God! You don't have the right to remain silent. Speak now, and don't ever hold your peace again!

# What Does the Temptation to Shut Down Have to Do with my Destiny?

Things have a way of leaking out regardless of how cold or frozen we think we have become over the years. You think keeping quiet about your secret insecurities won't destroy your marriage, but they will leak out in losing your temper unexpectedly. Others may think you are so good at hiding that, but even an iron wears out.

Maybe you have gotten far in the game of life when it comes to succeeding, but anything we bury alive comes to the surface. We must be honest about what we aren't speaking about before our silence destroys our peace of mind, wealth, health, and relationships with the people we love most. There is a time to be silent, but there is also a time to speak.

# The Temptation to Have Foreplay with Who's Not Playing

"You give me attention. You're
someone who understands my needs.
All rare but sensitive. Everything
I miss at home."—Cherrelle

Even Jesus asked the question, *"Do you love me more than these"* *(John 21:15, NLT)*. Jesus is God, and God is love. Why would love ask for affirmation that He is loved? When God (Jesus) manifested himself in the flesh- he experienced what it was like to be us. Because the LORD Jesus Christ went through the human experience, the Bible clearly states, *"So then, since we have a great High Priest who has entered heaven, Jesus the Son of God, let us hold firmly to what we believe. This High Priest of ours understands our weaknesses, for he faced all of the same testings we do, yet he did not sin"* *(Hebrews 4:14-15, NLT)*.

Jesus Christ, who is love, wanted to be loved. If Jesus wanted and still wants to be loved, we would be telling ourselves the biggest lie to say that we don't want to be loved. Crimes are com- mitted over a love that was lost. Babies were kidnapped by women who never had a child of their own, and who wants someone to love. The desire to be loved is so dangerous that many are willing to go after what or who is not theirs to fill that void.

## Don't Take What Doesn't Belong to You

I once overheard a woman arguing with her female friend about how she was treating her man.

She was reminding her that her husband is good to her and deserves to be treated right. The wife expressed her trust issues to her friend. However, the friend said to her, "You are going to make your trust issues drive him away." Then her friend said, "If you don't watch out, I just might steal him myself." That statement makes it clear that she is not a friend.

What amazed me about this conversation is that the wife did not even trip when her friend said that to her. Maybe she no longer cared. Maybe she already had somebody else. Or, maybe she knew her female friend was very flirtatious. Never mind, scratch that! When friends talk like that, it's time to question that friendship. Oprah once said, "You can't be friends with someone who wants your life."

Now, let me say this. Some friends don't walk up saying, "I want my friend's spouse." **However, everyone else's life starts to look**

> **However, everyone else's life starts to look interesting once we have given up on our own.**

**interesting once we have given up on our own.** Often, we end up admiring someone else's life when we feel as if we are stuck on our own. Stuck? Yes, stuck. Do you realize how many people stay in stuck places – thinking the only way to get through it is to look for playtime or a playmate to keep them company? Here are some examples of how we may try to cope with being stuck in self-destructive ways:

- Staying with someone we don't want long term only out of trying not to hurt their feelings by leaving while entertaining someone else across town.
- Not wanting someone who wants us but not wanting someone else to have them. So we only show them attention when we think they have moved on
- Staying with the wrong man because he pays the bills and you don't want to move back in with your mother just to hear her say, "I told you so."
- Remaining in a ministry that is detrimental to the will of Christ for your life but you don't want to upset your church family because they have done so much for you.
- Staying at a job that you're good at but hate and avoiding starting your own business due to being afraid to be out on your own.

These are just a few of the self-destructive ways that we negatively cope with the thoughts and feelings of being stuck. Feeling stuck is not a good feeling. It is almost equivalent to the feeling of being suffocated. When we are stuck, we feel desperate. Now we all know that desperate people do desperate things. While there are a plethora of examples I can use for this chapter, I will use the married woman in Joseph's life to exemplify the unfortunate opportunities that present themselves when we feel stuck.

## DESPERATE HOUSEWIVES

They say, "You can't turn a whore into a housewife." However, I would say to all of us that **you can't change somebody's needs by giving them what you think they want.** Keep in mind that in the old testament, many marriages were arranged. They were not necessarily the spouse they would have picked for themselves. This is "learning to love" someone at its best. What do I mean? Grab your Bible:

> *"When Joseph was taken to Egypt by the Ishmaelite traders, he was purchased by Potiphar, an Egyptian officer. Potiphar was captain of the guard for Pharaoh, the king of Egypt. The* LORD *was with Joseph, so he succeeded in everything he did as he served in the home of his Egyptian master. Potiphar noticed this and realized that the* LORD *was with Joseph, giving him success in everything he did. This pleased Potiphar, so he soon made Joseph his personal attendant. He put him in charge of his entire household and everything he owned. From the day Joseph was put in charge of his master's household and property, the* LORD *began to bless Potiphar's household*

*for Joseph's sake. All his household affairs ran smoothly, and his crops and livestock flourished. So Potiphar gave Joseph complete administrative responsibility over everything he owned. With Joseph there, he didn't worry about a thing—except what kind of food to eat! Joseph was a very handsome and well-built young man, and Potiphar's wife soon began to look at him lustfully. "Come and sleep with me," she demanded" (Genesis 39:1-7, NLT).*

Potiphar was a wealthy Egyptian officer, who worked for Pharaoh. Potiphar was wealthy, a protector, and a great provider. Nevertheless, that did not negate the fact that his wife was not faithful. Loyalty is not tested in moments of temptation when a naked woman or man is in front of us. **Loyalty is tested when we can be unfaithful but choose not to be. Loyalty is tested when you know you entertain a thought that you wouldn't want your significant other entertaining. Loyalty is tested when you take the person you know for granted to go after who you don't know.**

**Loyalty is tested when we can be unfaithful but choose not to be. Loyalty is tested when you know you entertain a thought that you wouldn't want your significant other entertaining. Loyalty is tested when you take the person you know for granted to go after who you don't know.**

## I Don't Know What it is, but it's Something About You

This woman has not seen a man like Joseph that her husband employed in God knows when.

He simply wasn't like "those other guys out here." Joseph was a man of distinction. The above passage makes it clear that Joseph is entrusted with everything in Potiphar's house. Potiphar respects the relationship that he has with Joseph. However, Potiphar's wife does not care about the relationship between the two of him. She wants him between her legs.

The temptation for her is that he is forbidden fruit and she is already taken. She is not going to leave her husband. She does not want a divorce. She just simply wants to have fun. Joseph was the right maintenance man. There was something about him that stands out to her. The problem is she thinks it was just his look, job description, and his physique. She does not know what it truly was. She was not aware that it was the favor of God in his life. However, she doesn't care that it was God in Joseph. She just wants the man of God in between her sheets.

**Everyone that says 'there is something about you', won't always respect what it is when they find out.** Joseph does his job every day with excellence. His boss appreciates him. He knows that she was off-limits. He remains respectful. Maybe other dudes were on her before him working in the palace. Who knows. The Bible

> **Everyone that says 'there is something about you', won't always respect what it is when they find out.**

doesn't say. However, that wasn't Joseph's concern. He did not notice that she noticed him. He did not want her and that was what turned her on.

## Distant Lover

The more he didn't focus on her, the more she wanted him. That is the mindset of many who have attachment issues. Many are attracted to those who have made it clear to they don't like them like that. However, that fuels the insecurities of many who lack the proper coping skills to handle rejection. **They don't see rejection as God's protection. They see it as a challenge.** All distant lovers are not across town or thousands of miles away. Potiphar's wife was right in the house with the man that worked for her husband, and she was crushing on him hard.

> **They don't see rejection as God's protection. They see it as a challenge.**

She was not thinking about morals. She wasn't trying to be ladylike. It was about to be a "hot girl summer" in her house. He might have been distant in reality from her, but she might have felt very connected to him in her head. She wanted what she couldn't have. Her husband was gone, and she knew his schedule like clockwork. Joseph and Mrs. Potiphar are now alone. She was ready to make her move.

# "Come and sleep with me," she demanded"

One thing you can say about this cheating married woman is that she knew what and who she wanted. You may be saying, "How can she know who she wanted when she is ready to step out?" Well, it's called "having my cake and eating it too." She does not do what some women do and quietly grabs or jumps on him. She wanted to talk. **Yes, temptation doesn't start with sex; it starts with the mouth. I call it conversations of the heart.**

> Yes, temptation doesn't start with sex; it starts with the mouth. I call it conversations of the heart.

## A Lesson on Temptation: The Conversation of Temptation

Temptation knows how to supply your needs. However, temptation longs to supply your needs through the wrong person or the wrong source. Temptation knows that we all have an innate need for affirmation. The Bible says, *"Good news from far away is like cold water to the thirsty" (Proverbs 25:25, NLT).* This is why many are attracted to the words from the mouths of those who are far away geographically or emotionally. In the world, we call that "whispering sweet nothings in your ears." Here are some categories of the wrong moments, people, and times of our lives to watch out for the Conversation of temptation:

## • Work Wives & Work Husbands

Trust and believe if you think this is innocent, you're far from Texas. This happens in the workplace simultaneously. Things are not right at home, and the best place for many to come to and the vent is the place you're stuck at all day: their job. This is a dangerous temptation zone because you're playing with your income, which could sabotage your career in the future, and damage your reputation. You may be saying, "no one my job knows except the one I'm seeing."

The only problem with that is the one your work wife/husband may get mad, "catch feelings," want you to leave your spouse/significant other and blackmail you. There is not enough hush money in the world to stop them. The holy scriptures made it clear that "jealousy is the rage of a man: therefore he will not spare on the day of vengeance. He will not regard ransom; neither will he rest content, though thou givest many gifts" (Proverbs 6:34-35, KJV).

## • Telling Past Exes About Your Love Life Issues

This is something many do. One woman said, "I only spoke to my ex because he knows me, and I know that he is going to give me his honest opinion." My response was, "If he knew you so well, he would not have cheated on you. He should have known how much cheating would have broken your heart." The real question is why are you telling your ex about your next? Are you trying to make them jealous, or do you need a listening ear? First and foremost, you don't know if they are secretly waiting and wishing for your relationship to last or if they might repeat what you said to your spouse/significant other when they get upset.

- **Talking to the Strippers**

Yes, you read it correctly. Studies have shown that most men do buy an escort, or prostitute, or purchase a lap dance from a stripper only for the conversation. People really need someone to talk to at the end of the day. However, when I use the term strippers, I am referring to talking to others who are lethal but are available. Be very careful. These are people that will listen to what someone else has put us through, then turn around and do the same thing back to us. Like the stripper, who is listening, only to get your money, these emotional strippers are only listening to get next to you and use your vulnerabilities against you.

- **"You Understand Me"**

This category is really dangerous. These are people who may share your struggle, background, past, or wounds. We often think they are safe to talk to when we are facing vulnerable moments. However, this is far from the truth. Just because the two of you came from poverty, a bad neighborhood or the same background does not make that individual right for you. I have even heard individuals who have battled drug addiction say, "I don't want to date someone who is on drugs themselves." What they are saying is they can't afford to place their recovery in the hands of someone who is just as toxic as they are. Now that's what I call accountability.

# "I WANT You, AND I WANT You TO WANT Me Too."

*"And Potiphar's wife soon began to look at him lustfully. "Come and sleep with me," she demanded. But Joseph refused. "Look," he told her, "my master trusts me with everything in his entire household. No one here has more authority than I do. He has held back nothing from me except you because you are his wife. How could I do such a wicked thing? It would be a great sin against God." She kept putting pressure on Joseph day after day, but he refused to sleep with her, and he kept out of her way as much as possible" (Genesis 39:7-10, NLT).*

It's true. It's so good to love somebody, and somebody loves you back. However, it's not always true with lust. Everyone we have a lust for doesn't always lust us back. Love is learned. Lust is what we are born with. Love is a decision; lust is a distraction. Love will make you sick but also make you well. Lust, on the other hand, will have us in hospice- thinking that we are in heaven. Mrs. Potiphar wants Joseph, but the young Hebrew adolescent doesn't want her.

One of the most dangerous things about lust for someone is that it can come off like love. Love can make you feel cared for, but lust makes us feel wanted. However, Joseph has to ask himself what I am about to ask you: Do you want your moment or do you want your future? Mrs. Potiphar was the perfect storm. If Joseph slept with her- he could keep his job, and lose his God. On the other hand, he doesn't sleep with her, loses his job, and keeps his God. Joseph has to decide a woman he didn't want or did he?

Now let's notice what the Bible does not say. The Bible never said that Joseph did not want to sleep with her. However, Joseph valued his relationship with God. **Sometimes all you have to keep you or get you out of the wrong person's bed is your love for God. Trust me, that's more than enough!** Let's face it, being a baptized believer in the LORD Jesus Christ and being filled with the Holy Spirit does not change the fact the flesh does not want to do right. However, the real bait of temptation is not the flesh- but the mind. *"For to be carnally minded is death, but to be spiritually minded is life and peace" (Romans 8:6, NLT).*

> **Sometimes all you have to keep you or get you out of the wrong person's bed is your love for God. Trust me, that's more than enough!**

When it is hard to say no to what or who isn't right for us, our commitment to the love of the LORD Jesus Christ should be enough to help us to walk away from what or who is not right for us. When we cannot find love for ourselves, we must remember the love of God!

> *"And I am convinced that nothing can ever separate us from God's love. Neither death nor life, neither angels nor demons, neither our fears for today nor our worries about tomorrow—not even the powers of hell can separate us from God's love. No power in the sky above or in the earth below—indeed, nothing in all creation will ever be able to*

*separate us from the love of God that is revealed in Christ Jesus our Lord" (Romans 8:38-39, NLT).*

## A LESSON ON THE TEMPTATION OF ATTRACTION OF SOMEBODY NEW

**I often say that they should not look good to us unless they are good for us. I have stated over the pulpit many times that we should not leave who we love to play with who we like.** Attraction is everywhere and it is not going anywhere until Jesus comes again. It takes maturity to know that that's all it is: attraction. Furthermore, attraction goes beyond looks. Have you ever noticed the beautiful girl walking down the street with a guy that may not appear to be all of that? Sometimes the attraction is more than the physical. Sometimes we are attracted to people due to various reasons. We may be attracted to how that person makes us feel. We may be attracted to how they think. We may be attracted to them because they listen to us. Or, we are attracted to them because they give us everything we are missing at home. However, if you are already taken, in a relationship, or married- everyone else is off limits. Now, if that last sentence turned you on and makes you want to fantasize about who is forbidden, we have to watch and pray that we don't fall into temptation.

Who doesn't like something new? Even God said in the scriptures that he will do a new thing (Isaiah 43:18-19). However, some of us are so insecure that anything new seems appealing when things have gotten old with the one we are with. However, what has gotten old to us is brand new to someone else. We must continue to find new ways to spice up our marriages. **Keep in mind that the enemy uses old tactics disguised as new appeals.**

> **Keep in mind that the enemy uses old tactics disguised as new appeals.**

## WHY DO YOU WANT TO BE A PART OF THAT?

Lela was 49 years old, with five children, cheating on her spouse with men in the neighborhood. Benjamin, on the other hand, was 25, single with no kids, and trying to get over a breakup. He ran into Lela at the laundromat. She noticed he was looking at her and offered to come to her apartment for coffee. He does not realize that he was the fifth man that she has invited for coffee in the last two weeks.

Well one day as he was watching porn, he noticed her face come across the screen. He was shocked to know that the girl he was screwing from the laundromat was an upcoming porn star. He confronted her about it, and she instantly snapped. "What I do with my life is my business. Nobody asked you to be here! I don't need you judging me!" She began to notice tears coming down his face. She has been doing this enough to know that she has him wrapped around her finger.

After four months of using his savings, his car, and using his house for a hideout from drug dealers, to who she owed money too, she felt bad. She asked him to meet her at star bucks to talk (She no longer planned on going to his house). After ordering coffee, the conversation went like this:

*"Listen, you have been making using you very hard. I like you a lot Benjamin, but I can't keep doing this to you. You are a great man with your whole life ahead of you. I am starting to see what I am doing to you. I am making you waste so much money on me, and I have a husband that loves me despite what he does not know I do on the side. I will mess your life up if you stay with me. I can tell you are used to girls who string you along and cater to your ego just to figure you out."*

*"Stop letting women like me do this to you. I know better but I honestly did not think you were the man that I have gotten to know. I have been using men since my dad left me and my mom homeless. I get easily bored with good guys, but you are too good. Please do me a favor and not allow yourself to stoop this low again. I have a husband and five kids. I get high and sleep around. On top of that, I'm doing porn. Why do you want to be a part of that?"*

Lela woke up after that. She checked into a residential detox center for substance abuse, looked for a good therapist, and started going to church. Furthermore, Lela got clean but also wanted to be saved. She repented of her sins and was baptized in the name of the LORD Jesus Christ, and filled with the Holy Ghost, according to Acts 2:38. The problem was that Benjamin was still into the woman.

Benjamin thought that he could play with the enemy and leave anytime he was ready. He was no longer in her bed, but she was still in his head. Like a moth to a flame, he was already in too deep. The downside of giving into temptation is one-sided affairs. Lela was wrong, but she got her life together by giving it over to Jesus Christ, her God, and Savior. Benjamin did wrong but no longer cared about getting it right with God. All he wanted was to be with this woman. He had an "If I can't have you, I don't want myself. If I can't have you, I don't even want the LORD Jesus." **Ask yourself; who are you willing to leave God for?**

Why is Benjamin willing to lose himself to someone who let him down easily? Do you really want to know? This has more to do with the fear of starting over or being so in love that he can't let go. The real issue is Benjamin has low self-esteem. The more a woman rejects him, the more he wants her. And please don't let him down easily! That's when he overanalyzes and thinks they are patronizing him (for more information on low self-esteem, read my book *Christ Confident: Finally Placing Our Confidence in the Right ONE*).

# Lessons on the Temptation of Chasing Rejection

There is an old saying, "You can't compete with a woman that a man won't leave alone." Nothing could be further from the truth. I would also say that one cannot compete with someone who does not want them and just wants to remain single to get themselves together and wait for the right one. Maybe you have been rejected by someone, who you think just simply wants to be with someone else, and they just won't come out and tell you.

Maybe they rejected you because, to them, all you were was a "stepchild." Maybe they rejected you because you remind them of someone in their past. The reason for them rejecting you is not significant. You have a right to feel hurt- but you have no God-given right to reject yourself. The worst rejection is self-rejection. When you give up on yourself because someone rejected you, that will hurt even worse.

My question to you is why do you chase rejection? Why do you want someone who does not want you? I will tell you why. You have made the erroneous assumption of assuming that you are inadequate and life is not quality living without them. **It's hard to detach from anyone that we have made our identity.** The Bible made it clear that we are complete in Christ alone (Colossians 2:10). It's hard to cope with rejection healthily without a relationship with the LORD Jesus Christ, the Almighty, who is our God and Savior.

When we have a secure attachment to the LORD Jesus Christ, we can pray for those who rejected us and wish them well at the same time. You are rejected because of the purpose of Christ in your life. In Bishop Hezekiah Walker's song, "God Favored Me," there is a line that says, "No longer do I cry when fake friends say goodbye…God favored me." However, everyone that rejected us was not fake. Some were doing what was right for them. Others just wanted to move on with their life. Most importantly, they found their purpose in Jesus Christ. Have you?

## I Don't Want to Lose My Job

*"Joseph was a strikingly handsome man. As time went on, his master's wife became infatuated with Joseph and one day said, "Sleep with me." He wouldn't do it. He said to his master's wife, "Look, with me here, my master doesn't give a second thought to anything that goes on here—he's put me in charge of everything he owns. He treats me as an equal. The only thing he hasn't turned over to me is you. You're his wife, after all! How could I violate his trust and sin against God?" She pestered him day after day after day, but he stood his ground. He refused to go to bed with her. On one of these days he came to the house to do his work and none of the household servants happened to be there. She grabbed him by his cloak, saying, "Sleep with me!" He left his coat in her hand and ran out of the house. When she realized that he*

*had left his coat in her hand and run outside, she called to her house servants: "Look—this Hebrew shows up and before you know it he's trying to seduce us. He tried to make love to me but I yelled as loud as I could. With all my yelling and screaming, he left his coat beside me here and ran outside" (Genesis 39:7-15, MSG).*

Many go to work to get what they are not getting at home. Many assume it is a safe way to fix domestic issues. This is self-deception at its finest. Countless individuals lose their jobs every day due to sexual romance in the offices. However, this is not why Joseph lost his job. Living for God made him lose his job! Joseph was a man of integrity, and his father raised him to believe in the God of his great-grandfather, grandfather, and his father- that is the God of Abraham, Isaac, and Jacob.

His God was the only God who made the world. Joseph God was still who he believed in despite the betrayal by his brothers. Joseph still had faith in his God when sold into slavery. Joseph still had a "for God I'll live and for God, I will die" mentality despite the confusion in his mind about what he was going through. Additionally, Joseph still had faith in God in the face of the temptation of the temptress.

Potiphar's wife didn't take that rejection well, so she forced the man of God to go to bed with her. Who would turn down sleeping with the boss's wife during the day when there were no surveillance cameras or screenshots that could be taken? Not too many men would turn that down. There are many who go to work looking for office attention on purpose. However, Joseph wanted something more than sex; he wanted to keep his relationship with God!

## Even If I Wanted To…

Any good observant individual, with good listening skills, knows the art of listening to what is not said. Notice the Bible never said Joseph did not want to sleep with her. Let us go over this again:

> "Joseph was a strikingly handsome man. As time went on, his master's wife became infatuated with Joseph and one day said, "Sleep with me." He wouldn't do it. He said to his master's wife, "Look, with me here, my master doesn't give a second thought to anything that goes on here—he's put me in charge of everything he owns. He treats me as an equal. The only thing he hasn't turned over to me is you. You're his wife, after all! How could I violate his trust and sin against God?" She pestered him day after day after day, but he stood his ground. He refused to go to bed with her. On one of these days he came to the house to do his work and none of the household servants happened to be there. She grabbed him by his cloak, saying, "Sleep with me!" He left his coat in her hand and ran out of the house. When she realized that he had left his coat in her hand and run outside, she called to her house servants: "Look—this Hebrew shows up and before you know it he's trying to seduce us. He tried to make love to me but I yelled as loud as I could. With all my yelling and screaming, he left his coat beside me here and ran outside" (Genesis 39:7-15, MSG).

Notice in verse nine, he reminds his boss's wife that she is off limits. Most of all, he reminds her that he could not do this to God. He considered it a wicked sin (This is before the ten commandments were given, of which one is "thou shalt not commit adultery"). Never does it say he wasn't turned on, aroused, or didn't want to. Keep in mind, the Bible already read our card, informing us that in our flesh is no good thing, according to Romans 7:18. Even if Joseph wanted to sleep with her, his walk with God was more valuable than anything.

You can be married and still see a fine man walking down the street. You can have a good spouse in your present and sabotage it with self-destructive promiscuous thought patterns and behaviors from your past. Nevertheless, don't lose who you have trying to get someone that you don't need. Joseph's present looked nothing like his dream but the God who was present in his life gave him the strength to resist her every day.

## RESISTING WHAT DOESN'T GO AWAY

The 2001 film *Baby Boy*, is about a young unemployed, bicycle mechanic, an African American male, by the name of Jody (played by Tyrese Gibson). Jody lives with his mother and is in love with his girlfriend, Yvette (played by Taraji P. Henson). Yvette expressed to Jody that she wants him to come live with her and their son. Jody is not trying to hear it because he was comfortable living with his mother rent-free. However, Jody gets upset when he finds out that her thug ex-boyfriend, Rodney (played by Snoop) has been calling her to collect him from prison.

When Jody confronted her, Yvette stated that she only entertains his calls because he was lonely and just needed someone to talk to. Jody snapped and yells, "I want a block on the phone tonight with your stupid self." Subsequently, while he ignored Yvette, Rodney crashes at Yvette's apartment, wanting to stay and get back into her life (he already knows she has a boyfriend). Yvette does not like him like that anymore. When Jody confronted her, she explains to him that "I didn't ask him to come… Now he won't leave."

The question is who is the Rodney in your life that won't leave? The real question is why was Yvette entertaining his phone calls in the first place? They have no child together. Maybe she was tired of Jody sleeping around on her and she wanted some emotional comfort, knowing that her ex still had a thing for her. However, we have reduced resisting to resisting sex only. Nevertheless, the Bible teaches us to abstain from the very appearance of evil (1 Thessalonians 5:22).

Joseph tried but he is a slave who has no power over this woman who is trying to overpower him. Joseph wants more for his life than the betrayal he is in, but the will of God has him in a place where he also is afforded the strength to say no. however, he was saying no to a woman who was the boss's wife. He was saying no to a woman who can get him killed without lifting a finger. He was saying no to a woman who still wants to sleep with him.

God Joseph is doing what your word says: *"Submit yourselves therefore to God. Resist the devil, and he will flee from you" (James 4:7, KJV).* The only problem is this woman does not run. She lives in the place Joseph is employed. Have you ever felt you did your part in keeping Christ's word, but it looks like He is not doing His part? Hear me child of God. Anytime the devil doesn't flee after you resist him, the will of God is behind it. So what do I do in the meantime?

*"In conclusion, be strong in the Lord [draw your strength from Him and be empowered through your union with Him] and in the power of His [boundless] might. Put on the full armor of God [for His precepts are like the splendid armor of a heavily-armed soldier], so that you may be able to [successfully] stand up against all the schemes and the strategies and the deceits of the devil. For our struggle is not against flesh and blood [contending only with physical opponents], but against the rulers, against the powers, against the world forces of this [present] darkness, against the spiritual forces of wickedness in the heavenly (supernatural) places. Therefore, put on the complete armor of God, so that you will be able to [successfully] resist and stand your ground in the evil day [of danger], and having done everything [that the crisis demands], to stand firm [in your place, fully prepared, immovable, victorious]"* (Ephesians 6:10-13, AMP).

## BLACKMAILED

Blackmail is defined as "any payment extorted by intimidation, such as by threats of injurious revelations or accusations" (Dictionary.com). The only caveat with this definition is that Potiphar's wife never blackmailed him with cash. In her irrational thinking, she might have thought Joseph will give in as other men do. This man was for real about his walk with God. Some men would get an ego stroke knowing that the boss's wife is into them. However, Joseph is not turned on; he keeps turning her down. So she decides to get a Plan B- and I'm not talking about the possibility of pregnancy either.

> *"On one of these days he came to the house to do his work and none of the household servants happened to be there. She grabbed him by his cloak, saying, "Sleep with me!" He left his coat in her hand and ran out of the house. When she realized that he had left his coat in her hand and run outside, she called to her house servants: "Look—this Hebrew shows up and before you know it he's trying to seduce us. He tried to make love to me but I yelled as loud as I could. With all my yelling and screaming, he left his coat beside me here and ran outside." "She kept his coat right there until his master came home. She told him the same story. She said, "The Hebrew slave, the one you brought to us, came after me and tried to use me for his plaything. When I yelled and screamed, he left his coat with me and ran outside." "When his master heard his wife's story, telling him, "These are the things your slave did to me," he was furious. Joseph's master took him and threw him into the jail where the king's prisoners were locked up"* (Genesis 39:11-23, MSG).

The Bible told us that we should "flee fornication" (1 Corinthians 6:18, KJV). Joseph did it literally. He ran out of the house because he did not want to sin against God and lose the trust of his boss. However, they say that "when a woman plots, even the devil takes notes." She was not going to let Joseph get away with turning her down. She was determined to take him down. She lied and convinced her husband that he tried to rape her.

For the most part, women are normally taken seriously more in these cases than men. Joseph had no one to back him up. His boss trusted Joseph, but a man cannot think straight when he is bombarded with thoughts of rage, jealousy, or just the thought of another man touching his wife, especially if that man was a friend or familiar guy that got close to. Joseph obeyed and passed the test! He did not give in to the temptation to play with Potiphar's wife. Consequently, he learned that she did not play fair.

## God Was With Him but Did Not Help Him

*"When his master heard his wife's story, telling him, "These are the things your slave did to me," he was furious. Joseph's master took him and threw him into the jail where the king's prisoners were locked up. But there in jail GOD was still with Joseph: He reached out in kindness to him; he put him on good terms with the head jailer. The head jailer put Joseph in charge of all the prisoners—he ended up managing the whole operation. The head jailer gave Joseph free rein, never even checked on him, because GOD was with him; whatever he did GOD made sure it worked out for the best" (Genesis 39:19-23)."*

Joseph did not need God to show up; God was already there. What do you do when God saw the whole scene of the crime of what happened to you, and he does not move? When we know that God is omnipresent, sometimes, that knowledge and awareness can be frustrating. It is frustrating because you want him to do something. I grew up in the church hearing the saints say that "God is right now God." However, that's not good theology. When we study the scriptures, we see firsthand that God does not always jump every time we call. He is aware, and can hear our cry- but the LORD Jesus has a plan.

> *"Behold, I go forward (to the east), but He is not there; I go backward (to the west), but I cannot perceive Him; To the left (north) He turns, but I cannot behold Him; He turns to the right hand (south), but I cannot see Him. But He knows the way that I take [and He pays attention to it]. When He has tried me, I will come forth as [refined] gold [pure and luminous]" (Job 23:8-10, AMP).*

Sometimes you feel like you shouldn't have to search for God; He should search for you. Job can identify with Joseph. He did not understand why he was going through what he went through either. The only thing that kept the two of them going was their commitment to the God that they served. Yes, you can be saved with unanswered questions.

Nevertheless, the Bible made it clear that God was with Joseph- but also made everything he did to prosper. God has Joseph prospering while betrayed, enslaved, and misunderstood. However, my question is why didn't God do something about the woman who lied to his child, Joseph? How have you ever had the LORD Jesus answer a prayer that you were not praying, but it seems like he did anything about what you were praying about daily? **Trust and believe, you have to learn to accept what God allows because he is about to use what hurt you to blow your mind and his purpose for your life.**

> **Trust and believe, you have to learn to accept what God allows because he is about to use what hurt you to blow your mind and his purpose for your life.**

## WHAT DOES THE TEMPTATION TO HAVE FOREPLAY WITH WHO IS NOT PLAYING HAVE TO DO WITH MY DESTINY?

You will be amazed at who the devil will set you up with just to bring you down. You may be thinking to yourself, "I'm not in a high place right now. I am still struggling, raising these kids by myself, catching the bus to work, and feeling like nothing. I haven't even received anything that I prayed for!" Don't you know that the enemy is not sending the wrong person to tempt you over your present; the fight is about your future?

However, you have reduced who you are to what you have or don't have. The devil is not basing your worth on material gain, a house with a white picket fence, two cars in the driveway, or the latest iPhone. The devil knows that your life is not based on your possessions (Luke 12:15) or the lack thereof. The devil is fighting you because God favored you. The devil is fighting you simply because you belong to God.

The enemy will use individuals who are broken, with narcissistic personalities and are using us to heal their wounds. The enemy will make sure that we have something in common with them. Don't get me wrong, the enemy will use people who are the total opposite of where Christ is planning to take us down. Why does he use any of the above, you ask? It's simple: we don't see them coming. We are so preoccupied with what happened to us, our current situation, or how far we have to go, that we don't see them coming. Keep in mind that the Bible made it clear that satan has transformed himself into an angel of light (2 Corinthians 11:14).

Furthermore, please don't harbor bitterness rage, insecurities, and unforgiveness in our hearts! That will make Satan's job much easier. The Bible teaches us that holding grudges in our hearts will cause satan to take advantage of us (2 Corinthians 2:10-11). Christ will give us beauty for ashes, the garment of praise for the spirit of heaviness, and the oil of joy for mourning (Isaiah 61:3). That is why we have to accept when Jesus Christ allows us to be in strange places and he doesn't seem to do anything about it.

Potiphar's wife will always show up when the wounds in our lives are still fresh, we are still vulnerable and the pain seems unbearable. Potiphar's wife will give you the moment of gratification rather than a long-term plan. Potiphar's wife only wants you at her convenience and turns on you when you finally decide to break it off. Potiphar's wife might not be a woman. Your Potiphar's wife might be a drug addiction, another man, past hurts, or old friends. Whatever it is, that temptation is not worth messing up your future.

Joseph valued his relationship with God. He wasn't even basing his decision not to sleep with her in his future. Jesus Christ was his yesterday, today, and forever (Hebrews 13:8). The Bible makes it clear that Jesus Christ is our life (Colossians 3:4). Joseph made God his life, and it appeared that all he got in return was betrayed. Is this how the story is supposed to end? To be continued…

# CHAPTER THREE

# The Temptation to Live in Regret

"I guess you always have a part somewhere deep in my heart. It's just too hard to hide. I can't get over you." -Maze

Many have said the worst place to be left is with your thoughts. Additionally, those thoughts can become tormenting, especially when they are thoughts of regret. None of us can outrun it. The successful woke up with it one day, The happily married couple even faced it. The thriving preacher even wished he would have never started a church. This is not a strange phenomenon; it happens to us all. Even the strongest man, with God-given strength, had to deal with his regrets.

*"Then she said, "The Philistines are on you, Samson!" He woke up, thinking, "I'll go out, like always, and shake free." He didn't realize that GOD had abandoned him. "The Philistines grabbed him, gouged out his eyes,*

*and took him down to Gaza. They shackled
him in irons and put him to the work of
grinding in the prison" (Judges 16:20-22,
MSG)*

He was not liked, but he was respected. He was not
accepted, but they envied him. God was on his side, and he
could not be defeated. This was Samson. However, in the above
passage, he finds himself in a jail cell for bad decisions. He lived
with regret for his choices. That he slept with prostitutes, played
with the devil, and told his secrets to a woman he thought loved
him. He never healed from his wife leaving him for his best
friend.

Now Samson, the man that used to conquer thousands of
men in a fight, has finally been defeated. He is no longer the
feared judge of Israel; now he lost his strength (which was God
himself) and made a joke of the town. Samson's regret went
deeper than regretting the wrong friendships, not speaking
to his wife when he should, and trusting the wrong people.
Samson's regret was taking God for granted.

## A LESSON ON THE TEMPTATION OF
## REGRET: DELILAH DOESN'T LOVE YOU

She is guaranteed to make sure you're comfortable. She will
be a listening ear. You'll never have to worry about performing
because she will take you as you are. She will give you the
respect and validation that you aren't getting home. She won't
stop you from going to church. She won't even text you while
you're cutting a mean step during a "praise break." However, she
will wait for you to get home to tell her all about it.

Delilah is not the loud, obnoxious, ghetto, and make-you-pay child support kind of chick. Not at all. In fact, she is a soothing voice in a loud world of chaos. She provides you with a bed to lay in and a pillow to rest on. Moreover, her favorite place to have you is between her silky knees. She wants you relaxed, and carefree and will make sure all sexual needs are met. There is just one little problem: she won't tell you that she doesn't love you.

Now let's not get it twisted. She will make sure that you love her. However, she will only give you the feeling that she loves you, but doesn't care that you love her. She will give you the cookie to get the cake. Your grandma warned you about her. You might get to court over her.

You might have even gone to jail over her. In fact, that is her plan. she will leave you in a cell of regret. I know she has a hold on you. I know she sold you a dream. I know you called her when your wife wasn't the easiest to talk to. However, Delilah doesn't love you.

You may be wondering, how can you tell that Delilah doesn't love you? Here is the dead giveaway: Delilah will always want more information about your life than she is willing to give about her life. The caveat is never to assume that the story she is giving you is real. Normally, she has fabricated a story based on your weakness to get you to talk. Yes, she will cater to your ego to figure you out. The reason why you can trust Jesus is that He will reveal Himself.

In fact, one of the benefits of being filled with the Holy Ghost is that the Holy Spirit will teach you all things, according to John 14:26. Jesus also tells his disciples, *"All things that I've heard of my Father I have made known unto you"* (John 15:15). Samson had consecrated, anointed secrets that were not for

Delilah to hear. **Here me when I tell you, stop telling Delilah what the LORD Jesus Christ told you.**

Here me when I tell you, stop telling Delilah what the LORD Jesus Christ told you.

Let's be clear, the Bible never said Delilah had sex with him. Delilah does not have to have sex with you to have you wrapped around her finger. She strokes egos and makes you feel important, and gives you a place to rest. However, you don't realize while you're sleeping in her lap, you've made your bed in hell. She knows how to make hell feel like heaven.

Delilah may not be a woman. It might be a man. Delilah might be a bottle of liquor or medicated marijuana. Delilah might be the boss who you think you have to sleep with to get the promotion. That is of minimum importance. The most important thing is that you don't sleep near or on Delilah.

Delilah does not like to go to bed when you go to bed. She is talking with your enemies while you are asleep. Delilah wants you well-rested while you're being tested. Nevertheless, Jesus told us to "Keep watch and pray so that you will not give in to temptation. For the spirit is willing, but the body is weak!" (Matthew 26:41, NLT). Stay woke.

## God Cannot Be Pimped

Yes, it is true that the man of God, Samson, was sleeping with a hooker. From a psychological perspective, Samson never had a chance to cope properly with his wife leaving him for his friend. So once he thought his marriage was over, he started sleeping around. Contrary to popular belief, he was not always this promiscuous. This is who he became after being heartbroken. He was strong in strength but weak in his heart. Although he was physically strong, the brother had a hard time dealing with his weak heart.

It has been said that "the man that values his privileges above his principles soon loses both." Samson was raised right, grew up in a godly home, and was instructed in the plan of God for his life. However, Samson did not value his God. Or maybe, Samson thought that he was a broken heart and that uncontrolled flesh couldn't be healed and helped by the LORD his God and Savior. What amazes me about Samson's story is not his strength, women, or broken vows. What is mind-boggling is that Samson never goes to God for help and healing.

Additionally, after the nameless prostitute he meets Delilah. Interestingly enough, Delilah is his last step before he is turned over into the hands of his enemies. What makes Delilah stand out is that she is the one woman who took time out to listen to him. There are many of us who regret not listening to our loved ones that cried for help. Some mothers wished that they believed their daughters when they vocalized the molestations. There are ex-husbands who wished they would have listened to their wives when she expressed a desire to get his attention.

Delilah wasn't just interested in hearing about his strength; she wanted to hear about his weakness. She was his enemy in a soft voice. Contrary to what many would have us believe about Samson, the Bible never described his physique- not one time in scripture. Bible movies and Bible storybooks have given Samson muscles and biceps. However, if Samson's strength was apparent to the human eye, then Delilah would not have asked him where his strength come from.

*"So Delilah said to Samson, "Tell me, dear, the secret of your great strength, and how you can be tied up and humbled." Samson told her, "If they were to tie me up with seven bowstrings—the kind made from fresh animal tendons, not dried out—then I would become weak, just like anyone else." The Philistine tyrants brought her seven bowstrings, not dried out, and she tied him up with them. The men were waiting in ambush in her room. Then she said, "The Philistines are on you, Samson!" He snapped the cords as though they were mere threads. The secret of his strength was still a secret. Delilah said, "Come now, Samson—you're playing with me, making up stories. Be serious; tell me how you can be tied up." He told her, "If you were to tie me up tight with new ropes, ropes never used for work, then I would be helpless, just like anybody else." So Delilah got some new ropes and tied him up. She said, "The Philistines are on you, Samson!" The men were hidden in the next room. He snapped the ropes from his arms like threads. Delilah said to Samson, "You're still playing games with me, teasing me with lies. Tell me how you can be tied up."He said to her, "If you wove the seven braids of my hair into the fabric on the loom and drew it tight, then I would be as helpless as any other mortal." When she had him fast asleep, Delilah took the seven braids of his hair and wove them into the fabric on the loom and drew it tight. Then she said, "The Philistines are on you, Samson!" He*

*woke from his sleep and ripped loose from both the loom and fabric! She said, "How can you say 'I love you' when you won't even trust me? Three times now you've toyed with me, like a cat with a mouse, refusing to tell me the secret of your great strength." She kept at it day after day, nagging and tormenting him. Finally, he was fed up—he couldn't take another minute of it. He spilled it. He told her, "A razor has never touched my head. I've been God's Nazirite from conception. If I were shaved, my strength would leave me; I would be as helpless as any other mortal" (Judges 16:6-17, MSG).*

Samson, like many of us, has taken God for granted. He believes that he could violate his Nazarite vows and still be in touch with God. Samson slept with a hooker and God said nothing. Samson touched a dead thing and God said nothing. Later, he slept with the wrong woman and God said nothing. Ultimately, he shared the right secrets with the wrong woman, and God said nothing. Samson does not pray and God does not stay. God did not want to stay where he did not feel wanted. God cannot be pimped.

## LESSONS ON THE TEMPTATION TO GAMBLE WITH YOUR IDENTITY

What I find intriguing about his dialogue with Delilah is that Samson was not unaware of who he was. Samson does not need to be reminded of his worth. Samson is just devaluing God and the worship that is due to him. The Holy Spirit is leading me to say to you that when you value worshiping God, it will deliver you from the trap of the enemy. Samson thought that he was somebody in God's eye, that it gave him the license to live recklessly and promiscuously. Many of us may not have low self-worth but we are living beneath the privilege of the abundant life that Christ died on the cross for us.

Samson knew that "God is good," but he was not being good to the Most High and to himself. He just knew that God would forgive him anyway since God is merciful or maybe he thought, "I will cross that bridge when I get to it." **Many of us have ruined our reputation at the expense of instant gratification without valuing our revelation.**

> **Many of us have ruined our reputation at the expense of instant gratification without valuing our revelation.**

Let's not forget that Samson had past hurt and betrayal by his wife, friend, and people that he never coped with successfully. He does what most men do, and acts it out through violence and sex. He was able to switch roles from being a man of God to acting like an uncontrolled man from time to time. Ultimately, he lost his relationship with God, and almost his "situations" with Delilah. The amazing thing is that he lost God and Delilah but only wanted God back.

The Bible made it clear that the fear of the LORD is the foundation of true knowledge (Proverbs 1:7, NLT). To know Christ is to want to know thyself. When you know who you are in Christ, you won't continue to tamper with your identity.

# I Was Committed and Gave It My All

Unlike Samson, who gambled with his identity in God, Joseph was all in. he was fully into his walk with God. He is not only in a literal prison, but he is also in a prison of a temptation to live in regret.

> *"And please remember me and do me a favor when things go well for you. Mention me to Pharaoh, so he might let me out of this place. For I was kidnapped from my homeland, the land of the Hebrews, and now I'm here in prison, but I did nothing to deserve it"* *(Genesis 40:14- 15, NLT).*

These are the words of a man who thought that doing right will when in the end, he did not understand how a family could be so cold-hearted. He thought he could express himself to them, without any jealous misunderstandings. Despite Joseph's plea, they refuse to hear him and sell him to Egypt. Potiphar's wife is back at home, feeling justified for her accusations against him. Consequently, Joseph is venting to strangers about the confusion in his life.

Many of us have been so hurt by people close to us that we have been too trusting of strangers. One woman in rehab stated, "After I lost my baby, I became promiscuous. I didn't care no more." **It's so easy to become so careless when we feel like the ones we cared for no longer care.** Like Joseph, many of us could see if we have done something wrong to someone, but it

> It's so easy to become so careless when we feel like the ones we cared for no longer care.

hurts differently when you have made excuses for them, defended them, and isolated your- self from others for them.

## "My Heart Can't Take No More, but I Keep On Running Back to You"

Then there is regret gone wrong. This is when we take a detour from the path that Christ has us on to go back to what caused the regret in the first place. This is self-sabotage at its best. The singer Ashanti had a song called *Foolish*. In the song, she describes how her heart can't take anymore because she is with someone who hurts her. However, despite the hurt he continued causing, she continued to run back to him. When we find ourselves constantly chasing people that have made it clear that they can care less about us, this regret is gone left.

## The List of Things We Have to Stop Doing to Chase People

I want you to pause right now and ask yourself why you continue to chase someone who continues to curse you out, talk down on you, and degrade you, whether publicly or privately. Why are you putting your mental and physical health in jeopardy for the sake of someone else who devalues you? Go through this list and see if these are things you find yourself constantly doing for individuals who are not right for you:

- Calling someone back multiple times who is purposely ignoring your call, although they are alive and well on social media

- Trying to talk someone into staying with you, who clearly doesn't respect or appreciate who you are and are evolving into
- Trying to get your family and friends to talk the one in your life into staying with you
- Watching multiple YouTube videos to see how to persuade them into seeing you are the one for them
- Texting someone who clearly leaves you on read multiple times.
- Using sex as a way to get them to commit to you.

This relentless chase will affect our self-esteem and make us think we are inferior to the ones that we are chasing. This relentless pursuit of validation will subconsciously cause us to detour off the path that Jesus Christ has for us. As hard as it may be for you right now, pray and ask LORD Jesus Christ to help you to accept the fact that everyone does not want to be in your life. **It's good to have a big heart but don't continue to settle for small efforts.**

> **It's good to have a big heart but don't continue to settle for small efforts.**

## A LESSON ON AVOIDING THE PITFALL OF FUTURE REGRET

As much as I love the LORD Jesus, I don't like waiting when it pertains to what I'm praying for. I am quite certain you don't either. One writer in the Bible put it this way: *"Make haste, O God, to deliver; make haste to help me, O LORD"* (Psalms 70:1, KJV). What really makes waiting on the LORD Jesus irritating to the carnal mind is when you are naturally impulsive. Regret happens to people who give up too soon or who react too quickly. Here are some things to consider to avoid the temptation to fall into the pit of regret.

For starters, know what the will of God means. The will of God is not a Santa Claus list. The will of God is about us walking out Christ's plan and purpose for our lives. God is not out to mess up your good time, but He wants better for us than we do ourselves. He doesn't want us to settle for someone who has married already. He doesn't want us to go after a career just because it's a big money maker. Neither does Christ want us to pray for just anything. That's why we need to be filled with the Holy Ghost.

When I don't know what it is that I should pray for, the Bible makes it clear that when we don't know what to pray for as we should, it is the Holy Spirit that will pray on our behalf. However, the caveat is that the Holy Spirit is only going to pray according to the will of God for our lives (Romans 8:26-27). God's will is not always what we want, but it is what will cause the glory of the LORD to rise above us. Remember the word of God is the will of God.

Secondly, our impulses reveal our anxieties that stem from insecurities (for more information on this, read *Christ Confident: Finally Placing Our Confidence in the Right ONE*). Anxiety is more than just a fear of the future or the unknown. Anxiety is about a lack of confidence we have in ourselves that we believe we cannot handle. In our self-doubt, we think that the longer it takes for the blessing to manifest, it will not come. Child of God, the Bible reminds us:

*"This vision is for a future time. It describes the end, and it will be fulfilled. If it seems slow in coming, wait patiently, for it will surely take place. It will not be delayed. "Look at the proud! They trust in themselves, and their lives are crooked. But the righteous will live by their faithfulness to God." (Habakkuk 2:3-4, NLT).*

Lastly, you aren't defined by what you are craving. You are defined by the word of God. The Bible makes it clear that our life does not consist of the abundance of things that we possess (Luke 12:15). What is the real reason why you want the designer bag, want to drop out of school to chase the fast life, or want to give up someone you truly love for someone you don't love but feel will make you look good? In fact, they shouldn't look at us if they are not good for us.

## The Ones Who Hurt Me are Doing Fine

The scriptures never mention Potiphar's wife again after she gets Joseph locked up. You see the pain hurts on a different level when you don't get a chance to see that individual again. Some of us get hurt and avoid people; however, others wake up every day researching ways that they can get in touch, reach, and spy on the ones who are far away from him. Joseph is hurt by a woman who is doing fine without him.

Let me ask you: do you miss the ones who hurt you? If the answer is yes, you are not crazy for loving or missing someone who is no longer concerned about you. What will drive you insane, however, is going back to someone who does not miss you; continuing to call someone who keeps hanging up the phone on you; fighting for a spot in their life while they have someone else auditioning for your role. Furthermore, remember to never let anyone audition to plan the role of God in your life. No one is God except Jesus Christ the LORD Almighty!

## REMINDERS OF REGRET

It might wake you up in the middle of the night as you go to use the bathroom. It may give you a rough start in the morning after waking up from a dream about it. It can make you want to take a social media break when you see them pop up in old memories and tags that you no longer wanted to be tagged in. I am referring to the memories of regret. I wonder sometimes what went through Joseph's mind in that lonely prison cell. Did he ever say to himself, "All I had to do was sleep with her." Most men have a different pattern of thought like, "I wish I never met her at all."

Many, for example, avoid going to the family reunion because they don't want to look at the child that they gave to their aunt and uncle to raise- knowing deep down in their heart that they were not ready to be a parent. Others have become bitter, living in a thought flow of jealousy and low self-esteem that they cannot celebrate what Christ is doing in the life of somebody who is a reminder of what they could have done with their own life.

**What happened to you or the mistakes you made**

> **What happened to you or the mistakes you made have not placed you farther from your purpose. However, living in regret of your mistakes or what happened to is not a shortcut to your destination either.**

**have not placed you farther from your purpose. However, living in regret of your mistakes or what happened to is not a shortcut to your destination either.** Sometimes it's not the devil reminding you of regret; it's Jesus Christ reminding you of what you buried so that you can face it, forgive yourself, and get on with your life.

## WHEN GOD DOESN'T REGRET THE THINGS WE REGRET

*"The next day when they went out from Bethany, he was hungry. Seeing in the distance a fig tree with leaves, he went to find out if there was anything on it. When he came to it, he found nothing but leaves; for it was not the season for figs. He said to it, "May no one ever eat fruit from you again!" And his disciples heard it"* (Mark 11:12-14, CSB).

Jesus walked up on the right tree in the wrong season. However, Jesus was ready to eat, but the figs were not ready to produce. Many of us are frustrated with people in our past because we came into their lives at a time when they were not ready for us. Others are secretly frustrated be- cause they are still waiting for someone to be ready for what they are ready for. Jesus was too hungry. He wanted to make sure that no one else who was hungry would rely on this non-reliable fig tree ever again.

Interestingly enough, Christ doesn't just walk away from the tree or ask to have it cut down. Jesus is so much God that if he wanted to, he could have blown on it and made it go away. He could have thought the tree away, and it would have vanished.

However, Christ does not do any of that. He cursed it instead. Why curse it? The curse was to stop it from producing. Are you trying to get out of someone and God won't allow them to any longer produce? Notice, it was not the devil that cursed the tree; it was Jesus Christ.

> *"Early in the morning, as they were passing by, they saw the fig tree withered from the roots up. Then Peter remembered and said to him, "Rabbi, look! The fig tree that you cursed has withered." Jesus replied to them, "Have faith in God. Truly I tell you, if anyone says to this mountain, 'Be lifted up and thrown into the sea,' and does not doubt in his heart, but believes that what he says will happen, it will be done for him. Therefore I tell you, everything you pray and ask for—believe that you have received[e] it and it will be yours. And whenever you stand praying, if you have anything against anyone, forgive him, so that your Father in heaven will also forgive you your wrongdoing" (Mark 11:20-25, CSB).*

Peter couldn't let it go. He just could seem to get over the fact that the fig tree really withered. It was withered because Jesus Christ cursed it. Peter is shocked almost that what Jesus said to the tree really worked. Did you really think that you could have peace trying to make something work that Jesus Christ the LORD has already shut down? Some of us really can't believe that the LORD Jesus did not give us the job we wanted or never give us the person we prayed to be married to.

Jesus reminds Peter that his faith cannot be in what withers. That is a recipe for regret. Peter must put his faith in God. Notice in the above passage, Jesus connects faith with forgiveness. Satan knows that if he can get us to live in regret regarding something that Jesus shut down, it will affect our faith in the future. This fig tree was misleading. Most Bible scholars agree that during Jesus' day, figs normally grew as the leaves grew. However, in this situation, the leaves grew faster than the figs. Many of us are living in regret because we felt led on by those in the past who put on quite a show and really had us going.

This is why we must not be so quick to trust the fuzzy feelings and butterflies we get over people because the heart is desperately wicked (Jeremiah 17:9). We must acknowledge God in all our ways so that he can direct our paths (Proverbs 3:5). **Have your feelings, but walk by faith.** Faith in Christ alone, that is.

> **Have your feelings, but walk by faith.**

What we must also take away from this powerful illustration is that the LORD Jesus Christ accepted this fig tree for what it could not do in a season it could not produce. We often have regret when we cannot accept that the people who we expect so much potential from are not ready to be what we want them to be or don't want to be what we want them to be.The fig was one of the cheapest foods back in that day, yet in this case, it failed to feed our very own LORD and savior, Jesus Christ.

I pray that Christ gives you the strength to accept what he has allowed. You have been giving into the temptation of regret way too long. You have been expecting others to have your heart for too long. You have been frustrated by others who don't see your best as good enough. You have lost weight, sleep, and sanity trying to make it work out with someone who is not God's will for your life. It's time to shake the dust off our feet.

## THE WORD OF GOD IS THE
## ANSWER TO YOUR REGRET

*"O Lord, you have deceived me, and I was deceived; you are stronger than I, and you have prevailed. I have become a laughingstock all the day; everyone mocks me. For whenever I speak, I cry out, I shout, "Violence and destruction!" For the word of the Lord has become for me a reproach and derision all day long. If I say, "I will not mention him, or speak any more in his name," there is in my heart as it were a burning fire shut up in my bones, and I am weary with holding it in, and I cannot"* (Jeremiah 20:7-9, ESV).

Jeremiah's regret superseded regret of the wrong relationship, not applying for a job, or embarking on an idea sooner. His regret was all up in the spiritual realm. Jeremiah's regret was doing what God had called him to do. This is where the enemy goes in for the kill. If he can make us regret the only purpose and will of God for our lives, we will go back to what can't or who can't make us happy in the first place.

I can identify with the prophet Jeremiah. Oh, the many times I almost walked away from my purpose and call because I wasn't always understood, wanted to just do my things, or not have to deal with people. However, like Jeremiah, the only thing that kept me going was the word God that kept burning in my heart. That's a fire that not even hell can put out.

Please don't regret the word of God over your life. When friends go, that word will be here. When people act strange, that word will be here. When feelings of inferiority are trying to make you doubt your place in the kingdom, the word of God will be here. There is nothing more in this world that I trust more than God's holy word. It was the word of God that created the heavens and the earth, and it is the word of God that will be here when it is all said and done.

## The Regret Starter Pack

There are a plethora of things that will make us give in to the temptation of regret. However, there are some key features that work best that Satan uses every time:

- Your adulthood doesn't match your childhood dreams
- Being Bullied
- Feeling like an outcast in your own family
- Telling your secrets and pain to someone who uses them against you
- Seeing someone else do what Christ put in our hearts but being too afraid to take a leap of faith in Jesus Christ
- Unhealthy Comparisons
- Waiting on Someone to Change
- Trying to impress those we think could help us get on our feet
- Guilt & Shame

- Over-Analyzing

These are just a few. Nevertheless, the Bible made it clear that weeping may endure for a night but joy comes in the morning (Psalms 30:5). However, what do you do when it's been a long night and you can't wait till morning? You're trying to give your husband a chance to come clean, but he keeps on lying to you? What do you do when you feel you have a call to ministry, but the board of bishops or your pastor hasn't released you?

Baby, you have to be Christ Confident enough to wait for your moment. God knows when it's time! Trust and believe that when the LORD Jesus Christ gets ready to elevate you, no devil in hell will ever be able to pull you down again. I have learned the hard way to trust that God knows how to tell time even though He lives in eternity.

## WHAT DOES THE TEMPTATION TO LIVE IN REGRET HAVE TO DO WITH MY DESTINY?

I never will forget in 2007, a member of the church I attended was diagnosed with lung cancer. I was her prayer partner and prayed with her as much as possible. However, one day, while eating dinner, and minding my own business, the LORD Jesus spoke to me. Jesus told me to tell her to humble herself. However, I was reluctant to tell her that because she was already battling lung cancer. Then the LORD Jesus reminded me that if she dies in her sins, her blood is on my hands.

I did not want to have to see my LORD Jesus Christ on the day of judgment and not have accomplished what he wanted me to do. I had to risk her calling me insensitive to her illness to say what I know Jesus Christ wanted me to say. You see, for me, my biggest regret was not being all that Jesus Christ wants me to be. At the end of the day, it is only what we do for Jesus Christ that will last when it's all said and done.

Maybe your issue is a regret of not standing up for yourself when you felt you should have. You may feel like a "punk" that you did not speak up for yourself. However, you must forgive yourself. Even strong people have weak moments. If you're not careful you will always find yourself trying to prove a point to yourself that doesn't have to be proven.

Or you may be living in regret that you didn't speak up for someone else. You're feeling guilty that you did not protect your daughter from your violent and perverted boyfriend. You have to accept responsibility, but forgive yourself even if your child is still holding that grudge against you.

Time is Christ's gift to you. He does not want you to live in regret over your past sins and self-destructive choices. If I would have allowed regret to hold me, I would have quit a long time ago. The enemy wants us to live in regret because he doesn't want us to believe that what Christ has for us is still waiting. So the warfare is to go back to what was and gave up on what's ahead. Child of the Most High God, the good old days are not behind us; they are ahead of us! It's time for us to rise, shine, and give Christ the glory.

# The Temptation to Neglect Your Gift

> "Somebody's future is held up by
> waiting for you to get over your
> procrastination to be who Christ has
> called you to be." –Curtis T. Bracy

Anyone who says that they don't care if anyone dislikes their gift, talent, or calling is lying to themselves. We all want to be appreciated, valued, and accepted for what we bring to the table. In fact, most kids who chose a certain profession did so because they were appreciated and commended for it. We indeed like to continue doing what we are praised for. There is more confidence in reproducing what the crowd wants because they love us for it more than they love us for us. More importantly, as long as we continue to give people what they want, we don't have to worry about shame and embarrassment.

Nick thought his mother would be happy that he tried to surprise her by cleaning the whole house while she was on vacation. However, due to a flight delay, Nick's mom came in fussing that he did not mow the lawn. Nick felt a sense of overwhelming shame and humiliation come over him that he could not explain. From that moment on, he felt the need to be a perfectionist or otherwise not do it at all. Little Nick was never taught that he does not have to overdo it to do well.

So when Nick is called "lazy" by his wife, he doesn't even react because he taught himself not to care about what she or any woman thinks. Caring about pleasing his mom as a kid made him feel insignificant and not appreciated. He loves his wife but doesn't care if she is satisfied or not because he will not let another woman hurt him like his mom did. You may call Nick's behavior petty or childish. Nevertheless, you may be doing with your gift what Nick is doing with his marriage: underestimating your gift due to failed expectations of the past.

## When Your Gift Doesn't Save the Ones You Love

A friend of mine was a nurse and was excited about it. She loved what she did. She went to bed at night feeling like she was making a difference in this world. However, that sense of self-efficacy was flushed down the toilet the day her father died in her arms. We will call her Destiny. Destiny was excited that she witnessed one of her patients, who was almost headed to hospice, experience a full recovery from cancer. Nevertheless, her happiness quickly turned to sorrow when her nursing experience and education couldn't stop her father from dying in her arms.

That day she felt an overwhelming guilt that she no longer belonged in the nursing field. Des- tiny said, "If I couldn't save my dad, who put me through nursing school, I can't save anyone." From that day forward she stopped working in the field altogether, went into major depression, and became addicted to alcohol. What happened to Destiny was she thought God gave her a gift that would save everyone she came in contact with, especially her family.

Truth be told everyone is not going to like our gift. Everyone in our family does not care that we can sing. Some of our friends on our Facebook page will press like when they hear we are hospitalized but keep scrolling when we say we have a new position. Everyone you invited to the party is not coming, but who told you to stop the music? The party doesn't stop because they did not show up, and Christ is not taking His gift away from us because someone does not like it. **So you might as get used to what God has placed on the inside of you because your gift isn't going anywhere.**

> **So you might as get used to what God has placed on the inside of you because your gift isn't going anywhere.**

## Not Even God's Gift is Going to Save Everyone

*"When Mary reached the place where Jesus was and saw him, she fell at his feet and said, "Lord, if you had been here, my brother would not have died." When Jesus saw her weeping, and the Jews who had come along with her*

*also weeping, he was deeply moved in spirit and troubled. "Where have you laid him?" he asked."Come and see, Lord," they replied. Jesus wept. Then the Jews said, "See how he loved him!" But some of them said, "Could not he who opened the eyes of the blind man have kept this man from dying?" (John 11:32-37, NIV)*

Lazarus has been dead for four days, and all his family members wanted Jesus Christ to do was stop him from dying. After all, isn't Jesus the life-giver? However, gifted Jesus shows up, but the family thinks that He is too late. Then there are other people talking about why he could not have stopped him from dying when he opened up blinded eyes. Jesus's gift to raise the dead had to be ignited by taking away life. Let me pause and say that God doesn't take something from you without giving something to you.

I have noticed in my own life that the LORD Jesus Christ has called me to minister to who I never thought I would minister. Jesus Christ will always call us away from the familiar. The familiar is where we expect the applause. The thing is that we "finally" get the recognition that we have been fighting for in the family all our lives.

Nevertheless, our gift is about God's will. That's what Joseph didn't understand. Our gift is wrapped up in God's will even when we don't understand.

*"Sometime after this, the cupbearer of the king of Egypt and his baker committed an offense against their lord the king of Egypt. And Pharaoh was angry with his two officers,*

*the chief cupbearer and the chief baker, and he put them in custody in the house of the captain of the guard, in the prison where Joseph was confined. The captain of the guard appointed Joseph to be with them, and he attended them. They continued for some time in custody.*

*And one night they both dreamed—the cupbearer and the baker of the king of Egypt, who were confined in the prison—each his own dream, and each dream with its own interpretation. When Joseph came to them in the morning, he saw that they were troubled. So he asked Pharaoh's officers who were with him in custody in his master's house, "Why are your faces downcast today?" They said to him, "We have had dreams, and there is no one to interpret them." And Joseph said to them, "Do not interpretations belong to God? Please tell them to me" (Genesis 40:1-8, ESV).*

## DAYDREAMING

Even in prison, Joseph could not seem to get away from his gift. Keep in mind that his gift got him into trouble in the first place. His gift to dream prophetically is what made his brothers hate him more. His gift is what made his family disown him. Nevertheless, Joseph finds out that not only he could dream in a house, but he could also dream in a jail cell. The irony is that he is not dreaming this time; he is interpreting the dream of others.

God strategically places Joseph in a cell where two men have dreams but are without interpretation. Joseph is not shocked by it. Joseph doesn't even say, "I'm through with this dream stuff." He does not even ask to be placed in another cell. Joseph does what many of us are afraid to do after feeling betrayed by our people who hated us for our gift. **Get close to people who can use the gift that the LORD Jesus Christ has given us.**

> **Get close to people who can use the gift that the LORD Jesus Christ has given us.**

## STILL HAVE THE GIFT BUT LOST THE FAITH

Joseph reminds the men that "Interpretations belong to God." **The right gift with the wrong interpretation will tempt us to give up on our gift.** Allow me to be crystal clear when I say that I'm talking about more than just dream interpretation. I'm talking about when we allow the toxicity of our past and the toxic people in it to change our view about the gift that the LORD Jesus Christ has placed on the inside of us.

> **The right gift with the wrong interpretation will tempt us to give up on our gift.**

> *"Simon, Simon, behold, Satan demanded to have you, that he might sift you like wheat, but I have prayed for you that your faith may not fail. And when you have turned*

*again, strengthen your brothers"* (Luke 22:31-32, CSB).

Losing faith in Christ over faulty expectations of your gift makes it harder to trust God. Notice Jesus Christ had to pray that Peter's faith wouldn't fail. Remember that it was Peter who would preach a powerful sermon, in Acts 2, that would ultimately and successfully result in about three thousand souls being added to the church. However, Jesus had to get Peter out of a place of self-pity.

Nothing hurts more than having a gift that won't help us financially. Having a talent that has not yielded a profit. Sooner or later you have to fight the discouragement of neglecting your gift. You have to fight back tears when you see others do on television what you have been trying to get notoriety for years now. Discouragement is the last person you won't see when you are tempted to wonder if your gift will get you out of the pit.

## I Used My Gift for the Wrong Reason

Back in the day, some women used the expression, "Sometimes you have to use what you got to get what you want." While there may be a whole lot of truth to this, there is also an amalgam of loaded heartache and broken trust as well. **Many have prostituted their gifts because they gave up any hope that they would be loved for who they are.** Gifts and talents often become manipulative strategies for those of us who have lost esteem and live in the mansion of self-doubt.

I have worked with young men who were involved in selling drugs but had the entrepreneurial mindset of a savvy businessman. What happened? They had a gift but gave up hope. They believed they were confined to their neighborhood, poverty, or dysfunctional upbringing. Often, when we give up hope, thinking that we are not meant to be who Jesus Christ called us to be, we use our Christ-given gifts for the wrong reason. Now the question arises: why did God give me the gift (or gifts) he gave me?

The gift and calling of Christ on our lives are for God to get the glory out of our lives. The ironic thing about this is that we are gifted by a jealous God. Jesus Christ does not want us to use our gifts and talents to draw attention to ourselves- only to Him. Your gift is a game-changer. Your gift is meant to get somebody's son out of the crack house. Your gift is meant to stop the molested girl from committing suicide. Your gift is meant to change the mind of your hard-to-deal-with spouse and your ungodly boss. However, when we are hurt, we are tempted to use our gift for the wrong reason.

## OFFENSES WILL COME

What can offend the gifted, one might ask? Many things can offend gifted hearts. However, allow me to list some of the most common ones that brake gifted hearts every day:

- **No Applause**

Gospel singer Helen Baylor is one of my favorites. She can sing her story in a way that confirms the faithfulness of our LORD Jesus Christ. She wrote songs about her past drug abuse, being introduced to famous singers, and even opening up for them. She even talks about how the prayers of her praying grandmother changed her life and saved her husband who used to be on drugs with her. However, she mentioned how she loved to sing the blues back in the day because the "applause said, 'I love you.'"

She continued to use her gift to receive the love that she wasn't getting elsewhere. Let me pause and ask you, are you using the gift Christ gave you for his purpose to reach others to get what you believe you are lacking in your life? Has your gift been used for the wrong reason as a distraction from past hurt, or trauma, getting a quick dollar, or betting recognized?

People do yourself a favor: **NEVER USE YOUR GIFT FOR AN APPLAUSE.** The same fans who clap for you will turn around and reject you. The same fans who follow you on social media will block you tomorrow (or continue to follow you to be noisy). Bishop T. D. Jakes, of *the Potter's House Church,* once remarked, "If you get drunk off the accolades of people, you'll die of their criticism."

- **Money**

What do you do when you have the talent, but not the paycheck? What happens when you have spent all that time in the studio recording only to be ripped off by the music industry? Yes, it indeed takes money to make money. Hollywood is full of stories of celebrities who have worked hard, and have even received a master's degree in their music. Many have left sitcoms in the middle of the season because they were not getting their due diligence. This is where faith comes in.

Temptation will whisper in our ears telling us to take a detour on the road to destiny because using the gift Christ gave us in a godly way isn't working. For instance, take the young gifted preacher who wanted to be used by God, but he lost faith because the pews were not filled. Subsequently, the young preacher backslides. He starts sleeping with some of the women in the congregation because preaching has become a side-job rather than a calling.

However, the damage does more than just hurt him. It hurts the many who wanted to know God but have a bad view of the church due to having an encounter with the preacher who used scriptures to get into their pants. Many have lost their faith in Christ and in their gift due to not having the means, resources, or profit to back it up.

Nevertheless, we must remember that our LORD Jesus Christ is the master financial expert. He was here before Suzan Orman came on the scene. Jesus is such a financial expert that you cannot beat God's giving no matter how you try. God can bless you without a loan from the bank. Christ has never short-changed anyone. He is not a crook. God pays fair, even more than we can ask for at times. the dollar is not almighty; the supplier Jesus Christ is.

- **Unhealthy Comparisons** - One of the worst insults to the LORD Jesus Christ and the gifts He has uniquely given to us is to compare it to others, especially those that we think have arrived. Regardless of how much we admire others, we still have to be true to who

Christ Jesus has called us to be. I have seen people get depressed clinically comparing themselves to someone or couples on Facebook who they never even met. Life begins when we appreciate the unique life Jesus Christ died, was buried and got up out of the grave for us to have.

- **Unresolved Issues** - Unforgiveness will destroy the gifted like termites. It kills us softly. I never will forget Oprah Winfrey, one of the most successful women in history, whose story of forgiveness. She went from poverty to passing out car keys to her audience on her talk show. She owned her network and continues to excel at great levels. Nevertheless, Oprah confessed a heart of unforgiveness towards her mother that she carried for quite a long time. It wasn't until her mother was dying that she chose to do what fame never prompted her to do: forgive.

- **Motives** - This one right here is right up the alley of bitterness. I have seen this one do an immense amount of damage. Many only want to succeed to prove to someone that they have arrived. Truth be told, some of them really don't care and have already moved on with their life. **Please do yourself a favor: don't miss the next move of God in your life by focusing on the people who hurt you that have already moved on with their life.**

Please do yourself a favor: don't miss the next move of God in your life by focusing on the people who hurt you that have already moved on with their life.

## You're Right Where Christ Wants You to Be

**The devil cannot uber who Christ is taking to destiny. Read that twice.** Joseph is not under the control of Satan. In fact, Satan is never mentioned in the story of Joseph. God was allowing his brothers to turn against him to get him to the next level of destiny. God did not give Joseph those divine dreams to allow his brothers, Potiphar's house, or the prison to destroy him. The Bible is clear when it says, "A person's steps are established by the LORD, and he takes pleasures in his way. Though he falls, he will not be overwhelmed, because the LORD supports him with his hand" (Psalms 37:23-24, CSB).

There were days in my life when I found myself frustrated with God because my gifts were not doing what I wanted them to do. I wanted to be at the height of my game, living in a luxury home, with cars, and the kind of life where I would never have to work again. However, God has never ceased to provide for me, make ways for me, and open doors for me. The Bible made it clear that we are not to despise small things (Zechariah 4:10). **The battle of spiritual warfare is not about your location as it is your revelation.**

You have to know that Jesus Christ the LORD God Almighty is with you even if you have made your bed in hell. If there has been one thing that the enemy wanted me to doubt more than anything was God's presence in my life despite the gift he placed inside of me. Oh yes!

You can be gifted and have doubt when your gift doesn't reflect your paycheck, standard of living, and your geographical location. Whatever you do, don't lose faith in the giver, and I am talking about the LORD Jesus Christ, the Almighty God.

## What does the Temptation to Neglect Your Gift Have to do with My Destiny?

I will never forget several years ago, I was invited to a church to preach. However, I was related to one of the members there. He reminded me that his church was not into preachers who yelled and flowed in the anointing of the Holy Spirit. I comely reminded him that they invited me because that was exactly what they wanted. If I would have followed his advice, the congregation would have not received what the LORD Jesus had in store for them.

Your destiny is waiting for your gift to arrive. If you allow the things that you have faced on the journey so far to discourage you, you won't finish your course with joy. The joy of the LORD Jesus Christ is your strength, but it is your gift that will make room for you. Joseph is spending his twenties in a prison, but little did he know that using his gift while behind bars set the bar high for where God was taking him. Let's see how much room God has for him. Flip the page.

# The Temptation to Promote Yourself

"Ego stands for easing God out."
-Anonymous

The streets call it hustling. Back in the day, it was called the grind. The world sees it as "every man for himself." Nevertheless, God calls it pride. Now let us be clear there is nothing wrong with working hard for what you want and achieving great feats. However, when we act like God did not help us out, we are right in the throes of temptation. **Pride in God's eye is seeking to reach for someone or something faster than God's pace and going outside of the LORD's will.**

> **Pride in God's eye is seeking to reach for someone or something faster than God's pace and going outside of the LORD's will.**

# The Sound of Pride

While many in the church world think they don't wrestle with this because they never smoked a cigarette or drunk beer a day in their lives, they may be guilty of the sin of pride. From a psychological perspective, having healthy confidence in oneself is pivotal as long as that confidence is in Christ Jesus alone. However, the LORD Jesus Christ wants us to acknowledge him in all our ways and seek Him above anything or anyone else. Pride has a way of sneaking up on us when we least expect it, especially out of our mouths.

Pride has a sound. Pride doesn't always kill, steal, or commit adultery. Pride is a conversationalist between our ears and hearts that it does not want Christ to hear. Allow me to just name a few things that arrogant individuals say:

- **I can do your job better than you**
- **I can have any woman I want**
- **Trust me, if I wanted your man, I could have him**
- **How come they don't ask me to preach**
- **Why don't they let me lead a song this Sunday? I sang better than her anyway**
- **You're going to need my help again**

As innocent as the above statements may sound to many, they are an insult to the LORD Jesus. Pride is a destiny-blocking issue. Pride makes us think that we have to come up with a get-rich-quick scheme because we are tired of low-income housing. Pride makes the sister who is tired of coming to the family events alone and being the bridesmaid and never the bride snatch any man and "make him" into the man she wants him to be. Pride makes the upcoming Pastor start stealing sermons off youtube to increase his membership- without believing the Bible when it says,

*"Except the LORD builds the house, they labor in vain that build it" (Psalms 127:1).*

## THE CLOCK IS TICKING

Cherese was thirty-seven with two teenage children but was never married. She always told her female friends that she was a hopeless romantic. In the past, her only hope for long-term relationships was learning new sex tricks to get men to stay. She never saw her mother "keep" a man and vowed that would never be her. She was a well-paid manager at a major corporation and couldn't understand how she could be so "fine" but so lonely.

Maybe you never felt like a hopeless romantic, or never had problems finding the love of your life, but there is a vacancy in your life that you are still waiting on the LORD Jesus Christ to fill. However, some don't realize that only the LORD Jesus can fill the real voids in our lives. In 2023 there is a person, place, or thing on deck to satisfy our guilty places, from social media, online dating, swingers' balls, drugs, sex, and alcohol. However, these things don't get us there quicker; they are just an adrenaline rush and company keepers that prolong our pace into our destiny.

Cherese birthday was coming up on September 28th, and she was tired of planning a girls' trip for her birthday this time. It was two weeks after the fourth of July, and she was not about to face thirty-eight without a man. There was a man at her job that was feeling her, but she did not like him like that. He was fifty pounds overweight and wasn't making the money that her dream husband was supposed to make. Nevertheless, Cherese did not want his money; she wanted love. She was determined to beat the clock.

Cherese finally hit him up one night after two glasses of wine and, he offered to take her out to eat that same weekend. She was not turned on at all but talked herself into believing that she was flattered. **You'll be amazed at what lies we talk ourselves into into believing when we have given up hope that what Christ has for you is coming.** He took her out, and she went back home to his place. He slipped something into her drink and raped her.

> **You'll be amazed at what lies we talk ourselves into into believing when we have given up hope that what Christ has for you is coming.**

All Cherese wanted was to be loved, married, and have children. She went to the hospital to get checked out for any diseases. She vowed to never allow another man to ever get that close to her again. Within five months, she purposely gained two hundred pounds to make herself un-attractive and as a form of self-punishment for feeling "stupid" for placing herself in that position. She avoided going to therapy and developed an attitude really fast. She was only trying to help God out because she felt God was taking too long to send Mr. Right.

## PRIDE STOPS US FROM TRUSTING IN GOD

You see Cherese was a church-goer, was on the women's department board, and drove the church van. She did not club around or smoke. She develops a drinking problem; however, as a way to cope with the discouragement of not having a man. She use to despise drinking because she came from a family of alcoholics. However, she was drinking to cope with the one area she no longer trusted God in.

Ironically, when we backslide, it is in those areas that we have stopped trusting in Christ's comforting Spirit, His strategy, and most of all His timing. Pride is a defense mechanism to cover the fear, hurt, and frustration that we feel about what we think is Christ's tardiness. Pride interferes with my faith. Hear me real good when I say: **To not trust Christ's timing is to not trust him at all.**

> **To not trust Christ's timing is to not trust him at all.**

## LET ME OUT OF HERE

*"And they replied, "We both had dreams last night, but no one can tell us what they mean." Interpreting dreams is God's business," Joseph replied. "Go ahead and tell me your dreams." So the chief cup-bearer told Joseph his dream first. "In my dream," he said, "I saw a grapevine in front of me. The vine had three branches that began to bud and blossom, and soon it produced clusters of ripe grapes. I was holding Pharaoh's wine cup in my hand, so I took a cluster of grapes and squeezed the juice into the cup. Then I placed the cup in Pharaoh's hand." "This is what the dream means," Joseph said. "The three branches represent three days. Within three days Pharaoh will lift you up and restore you to your position as*

*his chief cup-bearer. And please remember me and do me a favor when things go well for you. Mention me to Pharaoh, so he might let me out of this place. For I was kidnapped from my homeland, the land of the Hebrews, and now I'm here in prison, but I did nothing to deserve it" (Genesis 40:8-15, NLT).*

Joseph did not know that being favored by God would land him in prison. Many of us did not think that coming to Jesus would lead us to be heartbroken. Some mothers didn't think that taking their kids to church would result in picking them up from jail. Some didn't think that being gifted would result in one day choosing between their gift and rehab. Some with two master's degrees did not think that they would end up homeless. Some fathers did not think that their daughters, as they walked down the aisle, would be sliding on a stripper pole in the nightclub. I say again that Satan is a dirty fighter.

## SINCE GOD IS WITH ME, WHEN WILL HE ELEVATE ME?

Interestingly enough, the Bible made it clear that the LORD was with Joseph while he was in prison (Genesis 39:21). Back in the day, that was all it took to make the church break out into a praise break. All it took was a reminder that the LORD Jesus Christ was with us in the middle of it all. However, we are still getting through COVID-19, the loss of loved ones, inflation, family members on drugs and alcohol, and betrayal on levels that we never thought possible.

Furthermore, we have bills that need to be paid; debt that we need to be out of; hungry mouths to feed, and not enough money in the bank. We have been told to wait on God. How- ever, why wait on God when he is with me, one might ask? Well, **many times the place that God has us in is not to destroy us but to preserve us.** Listen carefully to this comforting passage in Psalms 121:1-8 (NKJV):

> *"I will lift up my eyes to the hills— From whence comes my help?*
>
> *My help comes from the Lord, Who made heaven and earth.*
>
> *He will not allow your foot to be moved; He who keeps you will not slumber.*
>
> *Behold, He who keeps Israel Shall neither slumber nor sleep.*
>
> *The Lord is your keeper; The Lord is your shade at your right hand.*
>
> *The sun shall not strike you by day, Nor the moon by night.*
>
> *The Lord shall **preserve** you from all evil; He shall **preserve** your soul.*
>
> *The Lord shall preserve your going out and your coming in*
>
> *From this time forth, and even forevermore."*

The word preserve is mentioned twice in verse seven of the above passage. Did you notice what God promised to preserve us from? For one Jesus Christ, the LORD will preserve us from all evil. The question is if God was preserving Joseph like He is preserving you and me, why is Joseph in prison? Why was Joseph sold into slavery by his own brothers in the first place? Please, somebody! Make it make sense!

Notice the passage never said God will stop you from going through evil; it is saying that God preserves you from all evil. In other words, God preserves us from the effect of evil. That brings me to the second reason for God preserving us, according to the above passage: preserving the soul. In Hebrew, the soul is the will, mind, and emotions. God preserves us from allowing evil to destroy our will, corrupt our minds, and play with our emotions.

## "Once I go inside, I'm Not Coming Back Out"

Most of us have heard this expression before. The above statement comes out of the mouth of those who are tired after a long day, and the only thing that will suffice at this moment is to be in the privacy of their own home, in their own bed. That means going out to eat with friends, meeting up with family, or even for an event that might benefit them. They are also saying if you want them to run an errand, or pick up something, speak now or forever hold your peace.

This is also true when it comes to the culmination of discouragement and depression. **A sign that one is traumatized by the past is the refusal to try again.** Many of us have been through pain so traumatizing and heartbreaking that we refuse to get our hopes up again. Now we no longer are moved by passion, love, or purpose. We have even given up on following the path that the LORD Jesus Christ has set us on. We are driven by bitterness, a victim mentality, and pride.

> A sign that one is traumatized by the past is the refusal to try again.

This is what psychologists call *Learned Helplessness.* This phenomenon germinates when we have tried multiple or few attempts to achieve a positive outcome, but they failed. So we taught ourselves and said to ourselves that it's not for us or we aren't meant to have anything or anyone worthwhile. However, experience may be a good teacher; it's not Christ's preferred teacher. Jesus said the holy ghost would teach us all things (John 14:26).

Never will forget in one of Tyler Perry's plays, one of his characters was hurt by men in a way where she purposely started to dress like an "old maid" to keep men from being attracted to her." Did she give up on love? Maybe not. Did she give up on someone loving her in the future? Absolutely. Fast forward, a man finds her attractive because her real beauty shined through the "old maid" attire. Truth be told, we cannot hide who we really are. If Christ gave you a heart for a person, place, or thing, there is not enough bitterness, rage, anger, or sadness to hide it. It's hard to hide the light of Christ on the inside of us. I would be here all day if I told you how many times I wanted to hide by gift and anointing and just be regular, but Christ has other plans.

The worst part about trauma is teaching ourselves the lie that we will never bounce back again or never recover. The devil is a whole liar! Life may never look the same again. You may not get your spouse back, and you can't bring your deceased loved one back. Nevertheless, the holy spirit does not want you to remain in that dark place.

## "Now that I am Out, Where do I go?"

Telling a woman in an abusive relationship to leave that man alone isn't always the best advice to follow in their eyes. Well, you might be saying, "Does she want to keep getting black eyes and busted lips?" Absolutely not. However, getting out of situations where we have ruined ourselves financially isn't easy. If she leaves him, where does she go? What if he holds all the money and the accounts and she is afraid?

Often when Christ calls us out of dark places, we have an immense amount of unanswered questions, loose ends, and consequences to face due to our lack of impulse control of not waiting on God to lift us out of that dark pit and set us on the pinnacle of success. By the time we decide to do it right (Christ's way), we have caused some internal and external damage in the process. What do you mean, Bracy? In the words of Kevin Hart, "Let me explain."

There are some men, for instance, that want to do right and be the father that they never saw. However, by the time they decide to settle down with the right woman, they got the wrong woman pregnant. Some women have finally decided to open up their hearts again and get married; however, by the time she gets married, she marries the man who loves them and not the one they loved but is pushed away. Also, for some mothers who are trying to be there for their children after years of drug addiction, their children don't want anything to do with them due to their frustration of her not being in the home but in the crack house doing their formative years.

Truth be told, starting over while still heartbroken is no joke. It can chip away at one's self-worth, turn you into a bitter individual (if you allow it), and even cause us to self-destruct, and even cause one to question our own sanity. It makes some want to give up on their own and wonder "why even bother?" I once heard someone say that one of the worst things a woman can do to a man that is trying to get back on his feet is to kick him while he is down.

## Interpreting Dreams vs. Selling Dreams

When the rapper Cardi B came out of the shadows and became an overnight success, the world was shocked. They were playing her songs in the gym, in the workplace, and in certain venues. Many were trying to figure out where she came from. Later on, after she climbed the billboard charts, she divulged how she had her money stolen by an ex, needed cash, and became a stripper. Furthermore, she also explained that she became a stripper to escape domestic violence.

Now there are many ways we can have this conversation. As a counselor, trained in the mental health profession, I can understand why she became a stripper to overcome domestic violence and make a name for herself and get on her own feet. As a preacher, I can say that she did not have to become a stripper regardless of how much she went through. Nevertheless, I want to use her story to show us that we all have a Cardi in us who just wants to be free, happy, and promoted.

Never say what you won't do. Say what you hope you won't ever have to do with the help of the LORD Jesus. Now before you brag and say, "Cardi B is not me, and I am not Cardi B! I will never stoop that low", think about the gossip you're spreading about that co-worker to get their position. Or what about you talking bad about others to make yourself look good? Maybe you didn't slide down the pole, but are you sliding into DM's to get attention because you feel your spouse is paying you no attention?

Joseph is not called to "sell dreams". He is called to interpret dreams. Joseph could have allowed bitterness to get the best of him. He could have said, "God has turned his back on me, so I am turning my back on other dreams." Joseph did not see it that way. Joseph knew that even in prison, "Interpretations belong to God" (Genesis 40:8). Joseph was gifted- not slick. He did not make up a lie to get out of prison. He did not manipulate the interpretation of dream telling for his gain. Joseph decided that God gave him the dream, and he was going to use it God's way for God's glory. There was nothing to discuss.

Are you using your God-given gift to your destruction? Are you using your intelligence to con those who you're gifted to help? Are you using your savvy money skills to prey on the naivete of the innocent? Are you using the body that God has given you to be respected, cherished, and honored for the eyes of many horny individuals to see at night to make a fast dollar to keep the lights on? In the end, it's never worth it.

## I Could have been a False Prophet

The beginning of 2020 was a beautiful time in my life because I had just met the love of my life the year before. I had landed a new job, and things were going well. Then came the quarantine in March. Everything was being shut down. To make matters worse, my job took away some of my job time. Additionally, the "cash-app prophets" showed up on the scene on social media. They were making money off the LORD Jesus Christ Himself lying on God.

Then I went on Facebook, speaking the truth of God about Jesus Christ and salvation, according to the scriptures. Then the enemy said, "why don't you just lie like these prophets do, and make fast money? God knows that you need the money. It's not like you would be out here selling drugs or anything."

I told the devil that he is a liar. I refuse to play with the holy word of the LORD Jesus Christ. Then the LORD blessed me with a great job, and he gave me favor with the CEO. You have to trust God when money is funny, friends are acting brand new, and especially when it feels like the LORD Jesus Christ is taking too long. If we remain humble long enough, God will elevate us soon enough. And by the way, I am still preaching Jesus Christ, the same yesterday, today, and forever (Hebrews 13:8).

## THE SECRET TO THE CHRIST KIND OF ELEVATION

You haven't seen competition until you have seen it right in the house of God. Satan's best strategy of all time in the body of Christ is to start the division. That division normally erupts with pride.

> *"But if you have bitter envy and selfish ambition in your heart, don't boast and deny the truth. Such wisdom does not come*

*down from above but is earthly, unspiritual, demonic. For where there is envy and selfish ambition, there is disorder and every evil practice. But the wisdom from above is first pure, then peace-loving, gentle, compliant, full of mercy and good fruits, unwavering, without pretense. And the fruit of righteousness is sown in peace by those who cultivate peace"* (James 3:14-18, CSB).

The above scripture reminds us that pride is the derivative of ungodly wisdom. When we live and associate with others who operate out of jealousy and pride, we bring swift self-destruction to ourselves. The LORD Jesus Christ is the kind of God that will only elevate the humble. The Bible makes it clear that God will save the humble individual (Job 22:29). Furthermore, while many in the body of Christ are searching for honor, the Bible is also clear that there is an order to honor, which is humility. *"The fear of the LORD is the instruction of wisdom, and before honor is humility"* (Proverbs 15:33).

## HOW TO STAY UP ONCE CHRIST STEPS YOU UP

Everyone who exalts himself will be humbled, but the one who humbles himself will be exalted" (Luke 18:14). God already had Joseph's step-up date predestined. God already knew that Joseph was going to come out with victory when it was all said and done. However, God was not going to allow Joseph's tears to change the date. God was not about to allow Joseph's unanswered questions to change the date. Joseph's date with elevation was divinely orchestrated by God. However, Joseph had to learn the God way that you cannot rush God's promotion.

Joseph interpreted both dreams of the butler and the baker in Genesis chapter 40. Joseph was still hurt but was kind enough to help the anxious mind of two of his fellow inmates. You would think that would move God to elevate him expeditiously. Nevertheless, God is the kind of savior that will let you help others and bless them right in your face while you feel left out to see if you will remain faithful to him.

Joseph was gifted but needed humility to balance out his gift. I have seen gifted people fall. However, they did not fall because their enemies, or God left them. They fail because they became arrogant. **Christ is not against us being successful; He is against us being prideful.** The LORD Jesus Christ wanted Joseph to be humble in a way that he would never stop giving God praise. **If God elevated you today, would you brag about yourself or about Him?** The only way to stay elevated on platforms, opportunities, and success that only the blessing of the LORD JESUS can give is to continue to keep a humble mindset, giving glory to God.

> **Christ is not against us being successful; He is against us being prideful.**

> **If God elevated you today, would you brag about yourself or about Him?**

## WHAT DOES THE TEMPTATION TO PROMOTE MYSELF HAVE TO DO WITH MY DESTINY?

It is true that whatever we do to get up we have to continue to do to stay up. If we told lies to get up, we have to keep lying to stay up. If we scammed our way up, we have to keep scamming to stay up. Many who have succeeded cannot enjoy the fruit of their labor because they are paying for the consequences of their impulsivity.

God is too wise to give us the right moment and embarrass us on the road to destiny. Most of our embarrassing moments are due to our emotional reactions which God is not to blame. Some of us have been embarrassed by the betrayal of someone that Christ never wanted in our lives, but the heart is deceitful and wants what it wants and who it wants. Nevertheless, we have to come to the point where Christ's will is what we want for our lives.

I was given quite a few opportunities to promote myself before Christ's timing, but I read enough of God's holy word to know that if I opened my own door, I would have to work twice as hard to keep it open. However, Jesus Christ promised that the doors he opens, no devil in Hell can shut (Revelation 3:7). If you promote yourself, you'll end up hurting yourself. If you want a real moment, let God do it. His promotions are sustainable! They will last.

So the question arises, "What do I do in the meantime?" You continue to do what God has called you to do, even when you feel unnoticed. I don't base how I am going to preach on the size of the crowd. I preach just as hard to a half-empty church like I would a packed conference. When Christ can trust you with little, He will make us rulers over much. I will leave you with one of the most powerful scriptures in the Bible that relate to promotion: *"For promotion cometh neither from the east, nor from the west, nor from the south. But God is the judge: he putteth down one, and setteth up another"* (Psalms 75:6-7).

# The Temptation to be a Victim

"If you let bad things stop you, you won't
be here for the good things." -Mama Jo

Now is a good time to remind you what the gospel is. The gospel, according to the word of God is the death, burial, and resurrection of the LORD Jesus Christ (1 Corinthians 15:1-4), who came to earth as God Almighty wrapped up in human flesh. Yes, God was in Christ Jesus (2 Corinthians 5:18-19). The good news is not that Jesus just died. The good news is that he raised Himself up. You don't believe the LORD Jesus Christ raised himself up from the grave? Check out this scripture:

*"No one can take my life from me. I sacrifice it voluntarily. For I have the authority to lay it down when I want to and also to take it up again. For this is what my Father has commanded"* (John 10:18, NLT).

What is my purpose in reminding you of this? Well! Jesus Christ, who is God, did not die to just raise Himself from the grave just for the sinner. He did not just get up out of the grave for the liar, fornicator, thief, adulterer, backslider, ex-convict, or felon. Jesus Christ also died for those of us who the enemy wants to be a victim.

## FEELING LIKE A VICTIM VS. LIVING LIKE A VICTIM

I believe that one of the biggest Judas we will ever be betrayed by are our feelings. Now let's be clear, God gave you feelings. Your feelings matter, but they are the byproduct of our thoughts. Feelings don't produce thoughts; thoughts produce feelings. **To feel like a victim, I have to first think I am less than what the LORD Jesus Christ created me to be.** What makes some feelings last longer than others is that we believe the negative thoughts that germinate the feelings that won't go away. To get a grip on feeling like a victim, I have to deal with my belief that I can be less than who Christ created me to be.

> **To feel like a victim, I have to first think I am less than what the LORD Jesus Christ created me to be.**

## THE CAIN SYNDROME

*"The man was intimate with his wife Eve, and she conceived and gave birth to Cain. She said, "I have had a male child with the LORD's*

*help." She also gave birth to his brother Abel. Now Abel became a shepherd of flocks, but Cain worked the ground. In the course of time Cain presented some of the land's produce as an offering to the LORD. And Abel also presented an offering—some of the firstborn of his flock and their fat portions. The LORD had regard for Abel and his offering, but he did not have regard for Cain and his offering. Cain was furious, and he looked despondent. Then the LORD said to Cain, "Why are you furious? And why do you look despondent? If you do what is right, won't you be accepted? But if you do not do what is right, sin is crouching at the door. Its desire is for you, but you must rule over it." Cain said to his brother Abel, "Let's go out to the field." And while they were in the field, Cain attacked his brother Abel and killed him. Then the LORD said to Cain, "Where is your brother Abel?" I don't know," he replied. "Am I my brother's guardian?"(Genesis 4:1-9, CSB).*

Now let's grab a few gems from the above passage:

- Cain brought God what he wanted; Abel gave God what God desired.

    There has to have been a clear command from God as it what sacrifice he wanted from these to brothers. Why do I say that? Hebrews 11:4 states that, *"By faith Abel offered to God a more acceptable sacrifice than Cain, through which he was commended as righteous, God commending him by accepting his gifts.*

*And through his faith, though he died, he still speaks"* (ESV). If Abel did it by faith, *"Faith comes by hearing, hearing by the word of God"* (Romans 10:17, KJV).

Cain represents many of us who, in our fleshly thinking, think we can bring God what we want and He should accept it. Nevertheless, God wants what he asks for. God does not want any of us playing the victim. Cain held back his best. We will always feel like a victim and live like one when we hold back the potential, resources, skill, gifts, and callings that the LORD Jesus Christ has placed inside of us. Author and poet, Dr. Maya Angelou said, "Don't die with an untold story inside of you." The story of Cain would have turned out differently if he would have brought the LORD what He wanted.

- Cain becomes despondent over something God gave him the choice to correct The story of Cain shows us the danger of not letting go. God confronts Cain, informing him that he still has an opportunity to bring God the acceptable offering; nevertheless, Cain is fixated on Abel, his brother. He was so angry and discouraged that Cain was accepted and God ignored what He told him to do. The victim mentality can't focus on the solution due to being preoccupied with the problem. I once heard someone says that "Consequences are decisions we have control over."

Maybe Cain felt that although God is giving him another opportunity, he might have felt like he would be coming in second place to Abel. Silly rabbit! This is not a competition; this is an act of service to the

LORD Jesus. **An opportunity from God never places us in competition with someone else.**

- Being the Victim will cause us to do things we didn't think we would do Cain ends up killing his own brother because he would not (not could not) shake the fact that God did not accept what he wanted to give God versus what God asked for. Cain committed the first murder within the first family. Cain never saw a murder committed. However, when we become preoccupied with feeling sorry for ourselves, we do things that we come up with things that we never knew we could conjure up. Even Romans 1:30 teaches that in the last days, many will be inventors of evil things. Cain killed his brother when he should have killed his pride, which emanated from his victim mindset.

- Being a Victim will talk us into relinquishing our responsibilities Cain kills Abel and goes about his business. He might have thought that getting rid of Abel would have helped him to feel better about himself. Nevertheless, he was sadly mistaken. Trying to kill someone else's dream, ministry, career, marriage, or household will not heal the pain that is covered inside the victim's clothes. God wants you to take the victim's attire off and put on the LORD Jesus (Romans 13:14).

Cain was now responsible for killing his blood brother. When God confronts him, he asked a rhetorical question: *"Am I my brother's keeper?"* (*Genesis 4:9*). Keep in mind his own responsibility originally was to bring God the right offering. That would have been more beneficial than killing his brother. However, the sad truth is that not focusing on the assignment that Christ Jesus, the LORD God Almighty, creates weight that we would have never had to carry.

Being jealous of someone else's life instead of embracing our own creates weight. Being who they want you to be instead of who Christ wants you to cause more problems. Trying to sabotage someone else who you see God taking somewhere will never work in our favor. I remember hearing the older generation say when I was growing up, "the unjust don't prosper." Truth be told, I've seen unjust individuals prosper, but it never lasted.

Cain tried to deny it, but God already knew it. That is what makes living like a victim will do. It will have us denying our role in it while blaming someone else. There is no healing in blame. Don't forget that.

## WHERE DID ALL THIS NARCISSISM COME FROM?

This has been a trendy topic for a few years now. The term narcissism is really another word for pride or arrogance. However, the truth about narcissism is that it is rooted in bitterness in the hearts of those who feel like a victim. Furthermore, they believe that the only way they can heal is by wounding others and playing dumb, and using reverse psychology when caught red-handed.

Psychiatrist Dr. Edward Howell gives us a clear and rich meaning of a narcissist:

> *"True narcissism is just not as common as it seems these days. In case the term is not familiar to you, here is a quick sketch of a narcissist. The truly narcissistic person is unable to give or receive love. They crave attention and need praise to fill a gaping inner abyss. The narcissist feels empty and disconnected. They carry with them no image of people they felt or feel loved by, nor do they carry images of people they loved or loves. Lacking what psychiatrists call positive introjects- images of people who love them, and images of themselves as lovable and loving person-they must live a life devoid of what sustains most of us. They are desperate and dangerously low on self-esteem, confidence, and a sense of basic security. But they hide their vulnerabilities because they fill them with shame. Instead, they try to appear better than everyone else. They fashion a false self to put on, like a fancy, tailored suit. They wear this accomplished, confident, false self to impress the world and assuage their inner feelings of hatred of themselves, hatred of others, and hatred of life."*

"They are a walking cauldron of rage at all those people who have not given them what they want: love, admiration, power, and prestige. They can usually keep a lid on the rage because they know it will cost them the admiration they so desperately seek, but now and then, when they feel slighted, they explode."

"They often develop phenomenal skills and proficiencies in the world, not to contribute to the world or for the joy of developing a skill but to extract to the world as much praise and attention as they possibly can. They seek to become a star to make up for how unstarlike they feel. They are ruthless in their pursuit of stardom because stardom means life or death to them. They need constant adulation because they die inside without it."

"The narcissist is deft in offering praise to carefully selected others to manipulate them to love them, but they mean none of it. Indeed, they hate those they praise because they resent having to carry their favor. They feel the world should come to them, and they detest the world for not doing so. When the world does not come to him, as it tends not to do, they mount their attack. They plot and scheme their way to the top. They are artful in moving others out of their way in order to take center stage. They are also notoriously vicious when they feel even the mildest slight."

*"They will attack the person they sensed slighted them with a ferocity far out of proportion to what the imagined slight deserved. They take delight in reducing others in their own eyes, as their kind of misery loves company. But no matter how much adulation and praise he garners, it never fills the void inside; his void is a bottom- less pit. The person who falls in love with the narcissist- and tragically, many people do because they are so charming- are doomed to a life of loneliness and emotional isolation for as long as the relationship last, using charisma, seduction, money, and power to control their prey."*

## SOONER OR LATER YOU HAVE TO ACCEPT IT

Normally when people call you for advice or counseling, they aren't in a confident mindset to receive it. They are calling you to vent before they go right back to who or what isn't good for them or to who or what they have not forgiven. What makes this frustrating is that you know this individual knows better, but their pride (not always their ignorance) has always gotten the best of them. **When pride is really at worst is when the creates a victim mentality causing us to think being the victim is what is best for us.**

**Believe it or not, life gets better when you accept people**

**for who they are and not who you thought they were.** Joseph has a lot of time to think about sitting in that jail cell for three years. However, one question that Joseph can't get away from is the question of confusion. This question is simply "Why?" While listening to another prisoner vent Joseph vents about not knowing why his brothers would treat him the way they did. God has given Joseph dreams, but all he wants at the moment to ease his troubled mind is an answer. Have you ever felt like "LORD, if you don't get me out of it, would you just please answer me?

> Believe it or not, life gets better when you accept people for who they are and not who you thought they were.

You see, Joseph's story is a story of betrayal. Betrayed by brothers who he would have never betrayed. He went from royalty to slavery within a short time due to the cancerous cell of jealousy that spread through the hearts of the men who were his blood. It's not Joseph's fault what happened to him, but it is his responsibility to let the LORD Jesus Christ heal his broken heart.

Here me good, I am in no way minimizing what Joseph or you have gone through, but I am also going to remind you that whatever happened to you doesn't have to cripple you for the rest of your life. Not when there is a God who sits on the throne named Jesus Christ who can take you from victim to victor!

## PREACHER, I'M NOT TRYING TO HEAR THAT

You may be saying, "Preacher, I enjoyed this book so far until you got to this victim crap. I'm not trying to hear that. You don't know what they did to me. I'm not letting anything go." Now let me give you some tough love: You are running out of time. You have been hurt, wounded, lied to, and betrayed. What you don't realize is that you are doing the worst betrayal to yourself! You are letting them win by sitting in feelings of self-doubt, and rage, and behaving like a victim.

The LORD Jesus has sent people your way that you've pushed away because they challenged you to leave your pity party. The LORD continues to give you opportunities that you turn down because you're fixated on a desire for revenge. You might have been abandoned, hurt, raped, divorced, or even left for dead, but the devil cannot finish off who Christ is not finished with. Christ wants you out of that pity party today!

## REMEMBER TO FORGET ABOUT IT

*"Not that I have already obtained this or am already perfect, but I press on to make it my own, because Christ Jesus has made me his own. Brothers, I do not consider that I have made it my own. But one thing I do: forgetting what lies behind and straining forward to what lies ahead, I press on toward the goal for the prize of the upward call of God in Christ Jesus. Let those of us who are mature think this way, and if in anything you think otherwise, God will reveal that also to you. Only let us hold true to what we have attained"* (Philippians 3:12-15, ESV).

One does not have to have PTSD to battle unwanted memories from the past and undesirable dreams. I have found out that it's hard to forget what we won't forgive. In fact, it's even challenging to be truly content within without forgiving others and our- selves. Not forgiving ourselves and others cause a plethora of mental illnesses such as depression, phobias, and anxiety. Let's take chronic worry, for instance.

I found it interesting that one of the original definitions for the word worry is "to gnaw." This is actually what a dog does to a bone when he chews it all day: he *worries* about it. That's what we do when we play the victim. We spend an immense amount of time and effort worrying about old bones that are buried in the backyard. Now hear me out. **I am in no way telling you to get over it; I am encouraging you in the NAME of the LORD Jesus Christ to get through it.**

> **I am in no way telling you to get over it; I am encouraging you in the NAME of the LORD Jesus Christ to get through it.**

How do you forgive something so devastating, heartbreaking, traumatizing, and shattering? Let me give you the true definition of forgetting. To forget is to remember your pain with a new perspective. God's perspective that is. You realize that Jesus Christ has a purpose for allowing you to go through all that you have gone through. When you began to study the word of God and ask God to fill you with the Holy Spirit, He will reveal to you his purpose and will for your life. You know what. Let's talk about the Holy Spirit.

## HELP FROM THE HOLY SPIRIT

*"And the Holy Spirit helps us in our weakness.*
*For example, we don't know what God wants*
*us to pray for. But the Holy Spirit prays for us*

*with groanings that cannot be expressed in words. And the Father who knows all hearts knows what the Spirit is saying, for the Spirit pleads for us believers in harmony with God's own will. And we know that God causes everything to work together for the good of those who love God and are called according to his purpose for them. For God knew his people in advance, and he chose them to become like his Son, so that his Son would be the firstborn among many brothers and sisters. And having chosen them, he called them to come to him. And having called them, he gave them right standing with himself. And having given them right standing, he gave them his glory. What shall we say about such wonderful things as these? If God is for us, who can ever be against us"* (Romans 8:26-31, NLT)?

When we have been hurt and scared by people that we love, wounded and abandoned by those we respected, shocked and shattered by the friends and family we counted on, it is like walking in on a crime scene. Where do we begin? Who do I talk to? Who can I run to? What didn't see it coming? I would like to call the above passage the victim packet. Why? Let's take a few gems from the above victim packet if we are going to go from being victims to living as victors.

- **Give Up the "Got Everybody Figured Out Mentality"**

When we have been wounded, left, betrayed, scared, and taken advantage of, we teach Ourselves how to cope with pain in negative ways that ultimately sabotage our present and future. For instance, a woman devotes her life to a man that she loves, who cheated on her. While she has the right to be hurt, to cry, and even feel strong urges of rage, tempting her to react out of impulse, she is playing the victim by thinking she has all men figured out. Hear me real good: Being hurt does not make us a victim- it makes us human. Reacting out of toxic thinking does.

Romans 8:26 made it clear that we need the Holy Spirit to pray for us. This scripture carries so much weight to it because it reminds me that when I pray during my feelings of vulnerability, I may not be asking God for what I need, but what my weakness and pain think I want. However, the Holy Ghost loves me so, that He will pray the will of God for my life. Give up the self-sabotaging wisdom that you think you have and trust the wisdom of the Holy Spirit to guide you into all truth (John 14:26).

- **You MUST trust the Will of God over Your Will for Revenge**

Joseph could have done what some Christians do out of ignorance and that is prey against his brothers while praying about them. No. Joseph knew better. As Apostle, Dr. C. A. Cowart of the Churches of God the Bibleway Inc, put it "You can't treat people like dirt and still be clean." Trust God when He allows your enemies to live. Be faithful to him when he allows the perpetrator to be blessed because Christ will let them live long enough to see you prosper. However, their success will be short-lived. Haven't you read Psalms Chapter 1?

*"Blessed is the man*
*Who walks not in the counsel of the ungodly,*
*Nor stands in the path of sinners,*

*Nor sits in the seat of the scornful;*
*But his delight is in the law of the* LORD,
*And in His law he meditates day and night.*
*He shall be like a tree*
*Planted by the rivers of water,*
*That brings forth its fruit in its season,*
*Whose leaf also shall not wither;*
*And whatever he does shall prosper.*
*The ungodly are not so,*
*But are like the chaff which the wind drives away.*
*Therefore the ungodly shall not stand in the judgment,*
*Nor sinners in the congregation of the righteous.*
*For the* LORD *knows the way of the righteous,*
*But the way of the ungodly shall perish"* (NKJV).

## • **You are in Good Standing with Christ**

Regardless of who neglected, abandoned, or rejected you, you are in good standing with the LORD Jesus Christ once you truly repent of your sins, are baptized in the name of the LORD Jesus Christ and filled with the Holy Ghost (Acts 2:38). You may always be the black sheep of the family, the outcast at work, and the accused when you were one hundred percent innocent. Nevertheless, regardless of what clique you are kicked out of, nobody can separate you from the love of the LORD Jesus Christ, and I mean absolutely, positively nobody! To receive the glory of God in our lives is to be in the right standing with God.

## • **God is for You**

You are not an accident. You are not a mistake. I don't care if you were born out of a rape or molestation. I don't care if they found you in a trash can, you are royalty to the LORD Jesus Christ. Hold that hung-down head of yours up, and act like Jesus died, was buried, and risen for you. You are more than a conqueror through the LORD Jesus Christ that loves you. Might I remind you that Jesus loves you with everlasting love, according to Jeremiah 31:3.

## You're Doing it Again

It takes a lot of patience to work with those who have been wounded, hurt, lied to, and betrayed. They don't take kindly to people telling them to "get over it," or "life goes on," or "somebody had it worse than you." Finally is the "you think you the only one who's been hurt?" question. **We really should be encouraging them to get through it- not get over it.**

> **We really should be encouraging them to get through it- not get over it.**

Unfortunately, time does not heal all wounds. Nevertheless, the LORD Jesus Christ God Almighty, is the healer of the broken-hearted (Luke 4:18). However, what do you do when you're wounded by a Christ wound? What do I mean by that? Joseph is in trouble, betrayed by his brothers, and placed in prison over a gift God gave him. What do you do when it hurts to be you?

Many of us have been healed by the LORD Jesus but refuse to embrace the healing because we got our hearts healed but didn't renew our minds. Healing requires follow-up visits to the word of God daily to renew the mind. No wonder the psalmist David asks God to *"Order my steps in thy word: and let not any iniquity have dominion over me"* (Psalms 119:133, KJV).

Let me give you an example of what I mean. Take Morris, for instance, who was traumatized by being left in the bathroom for hours after being beaten by his father daily.

He grows up not trusting people and developing claustrophobia (fear of closed spaces).

Overtime, he picks up a drug addiction to deal with the pain he never asked God to heal.

Then he gets married and is influenced by his wife to go to church. At first, he was reluctant due to a distrust of preachers because the father that locked him in the dark bathroom for hours was a Pastor.

Subsequently, after getting arrested for a DWI, and being convicted. He is placed in solitary confinement for several angry outbursts with other inmates. Being in that hole causes him to relive those moments when he had been traumatized by what his father did.

At that moment, he cried out to the LORD Jesus and was filled with the Holy Spirit, speaking in tongues as the Spirit gave him utterance.

Subsequently, as he is enjoying his walk with the LORD, he gets a phone call that his father was dying of prostate cancer. Morris feels bad but refuses to go see his dad for all that his father did to him. Although Morris was a blood-washed believer, he has not allowed the LORD Jesus Christ to heal his pain. **It's not enough to invite Christ into your heart and not allow Him to heal the pain in your heart.**

> **It's not enough to invite Christ into your heart and not allow Him to heal the pain in your heart.**

Because he never learned how to open up about his pain, Morris relapsed and went back to drinking alcohol while still attending church faithfully. Church will become routine when we don't trust Christ with our secrets and our past hurts. His wife informed Morris that she would go stay at a hotel if he doesn't go to rehab. Morris checked himself into treatment. However, it was a detox treatment rehab in Florida where his dying father lived. He made up his mind that forgiveness is only something that the victorious can do- not the victim.

## THEY DON'T CARE ABOUT WHAT THEY DID TO ME

Truth be told, some people aren't sorry nor do they care about the heartbreak that they have caused you. Furthermore, some of them really didn't think you would be affected by what they did to you. The man who left you for another woman may be happily married across town with another woman - not thinking about you. The siblings that didn't even tell you that your mother was sick- but only reached out to you for the funeral didn't even apologize. The co-worker who got you fired while you're collecting unemployment may still be gossiping about you currently.

However, you must know that all that pain, hurt, and bitterness you carry will become a weight that you don't have to carry. I know it's easy to sit in the car after you park and think about how they did you. It's easy to push the loyal ones away because of the betrayal of those who you thought were loyal. It's even easier to let depression, anxiety, fear, hurt, and frustration build a cave around you for the rest of your life. Nevertheless, you aren't reading this book by accident. The LORD Jesus Christ is calling you out of that cave right now in the NAME of Jesus.

They may not care. They probably will never say sorry, but you have to refuse to lie down and die. My Bible declares, *"I shall not die, but I shall live, and recount the deeds of the LORD"* (Psalms 118:17, ESV). Christ sees your tears, and God knows that they don't care, but Jesus Christ wants you to *"Give all your worries to God, for he cares about you"* (1 Peter 5:7, NLT). Please resist the temptation to be a victim because the LORD Jesus Christ has never left you, despite what they did to you.

## *WE HAVE OUR FAULTS TOO*

Now, this part can not be easy to hear, but we have our faults as well. Listen to this scripture that is seldom taught or preached:

> *"Don't pay attention to everything people say,*
> *or you may hear your servant cursing you.*
> *for in your heart you know that many times*
> *you yourself have cursed others"* (Ecclesiastes
> 7:21-22, CSB).

Yes, it is very true that "hurt people hurt people." We have to remember that people cannot give us what they don't have. The person you want an apology from is probably waiting on an apology from someone else in their life. The person who has been mean as a snake to you is truly not happy inside. When people have secretly given up hope, they act very cold. Show them mercy because we need Christ's mercy every day of our lives.

## WHAT DOES THE TEMPTATION TO PLAY THE VICTIM HAVE TO DO WITH MY DESTINY?

Playing the role of the victim is a time waster. Playing the victim causes us to forget that if God has allowed us to go through this, there must be glory on the other side of this. You don't want to be talking about who did you wrong till you are old and gray sitting in the nursing home when you could have spent all that time in your life walking in your calling.

Now here me good with your spiritual ear- not just your natural ear when I say this: the person who hurt you did not waste your time because God is their puppet master. You are wasting your time by not trusting the puppet master, the LORD Jesus Christ God almighty himself. Haven't you realized that the people who hurt you really think that God is on their side, but you are wasting time not realizing that Christ is on yours?

# The Temptation to Finally Get Even

"The only people you should
get even with are those who
helped you." -John Southard

My grandmother was my heart. She took me in when I was five years old. She did not take me in because my mother wasn't around. My mother worked hard to put my brother and I through school. However, my grandmother didn't mind helping out. I can remember this like yesterday. I went to visit my grandmother one day and never went back home. My grandmother loved me unconditionally regardless of what people told her about me. Most importantly, she taught me about the LORD Jesus Christ.

She encouraged me to have a relationship with God, to read the Bible daily, and live right. She taught me how to take care of myself, save money, cook, and treat a woman. I think about her every day of my life. She was unforgettable in every way. However, the best lessons that she taught were not verbal but demonstrated in how she responded to her enemies, even when they were her own flesh and blood.

I watched my grandmother cry in her own house for many days over how people treated her. However, most of those tears were over her own people. The people who she thought would never betray or do her wrong. She was hurt, shocked, and even depressed about it. However, she knew there was only one way to respond: with love. That made me mad every single time.

You see, I called myself her protector. I wanted to protect her physically and also emotionally. So if someone looked like they were about to get smart, I was already ready to give them the business. See I am the kind of person, you can come for me. I'll be good. However, I'm protective of my family. If there was one thing my grandmother stayed on me about, it was treating people who treated her wrong, right. There was an occasion when someone had her in tears. I was ready to go after that person with a vengeance. I never will forget her response to me as she lay in the hospital room: "Baby, God is using you too much." Then there was another occasion where that same person rubbed me the wrong way, and I let that individual have it. When I told my grandmother what happened, she said to me, "You should have kept walking."

## HAVE TRUTH TELLERS IN YOUR LIFE

I once heard someone say, "a good friend doesn't sound like a good friend when they are telling you what is wrong with you." Many times, friends or family don't call the truth-tellers when they mess up because they know they are going to get the truth, the whole truth, and nothing but the truth. Truth tellers, however, should speak the truth in love, according to Ephesians 4:13. Furthermore, truth-tellers don't just confront us about our mistakes, they also remind us that the temptations we are phasing now are trying to destroy us before we get to our future.

Temptation hates the truth. I mean it really hates the truth. Why? We have to lie to ourselves to satisfy the yearning and impulsive cravings of our lust. Yes, revenge-seeking may not sound as attractive as sex or secrets. However, there are many that have never stepped out on their spouse, ever became addicted to illicit substances, or have had a gambling problem that kept them in Vegas every weekend. Some of us can care less about a needle in our arm, the fragrance of another woman, or getting money illegally.

Some of us eat, sleep, and think of revenge. It's on our bucket list. We are constantly, waiting for the day that we can see them again in person, and let them have it. Yes, even in the face of all the success that the LORD Jesus Christ has already afforded us, we are not enjoying that as much as we are the evil thoughts of the imagination of the heart that screams for revenge.

The Bible is quite clear that Joseph is not looking for revenge. He may not be able to locate the brothers that wanted to get rid of him, but Joseph knows where to find his integrity. You heard what he told Potiphar's wife when she went to cheat on her husband: "How can I do this great evil and sin against God" (Genesis 39:9, NASB)? Joseph may not know why this has all happened to him, but he knows his God operates in truth.

Joseph has no friends telling him to hang in there. He has no loved one encouraging him to hold to God's unchanging hand. No Joseph has no support system in place. He is holding on to his integrity. He chooses to live in truth while his brothers are living a lie, making their father think that he is dead (Genesis 37:31-36). What do you do when a lie is enjoying life on one side of town while you're walking in truth on the other side of town?

## A LITTLE NOTE ON TEMPTATION VS. TRUTH

One day, Truth went swimming and left his shirt on the shore. While Truth was in the water enjoying his swim, Lie came and took Truth's clothes and went around looking like Truth. After forty-five minutes, Truth came out of the water and noticed Lie with his clothes on, walking around looking like him. Truth was hurt but made up his mind. Truth said to himself, "I know what Lie wants me to do. He wants me to go around looking like him and embarrass myself. I am going to go everywhere Lie went with no clothes on. I am hurt, but I am going to walk around as the Naked Truth."

When we are hurting, crying, stressing, losing sleep, and having our job production go down because we are confused, it seems like only revenge will numb the pain. How- ever, Jesus Christ has you reading this book for a reason. You can be hurt and keep your character but sweet ole revenge is something that you have to step outside of your identity and the will of God to step into. Nevertheless, the LORD Jesus Christ does not want us to walk outside of His word to get revenge. Christ said, *"If you continue in*

> *My word, then you are truly disciples of Mine;*
> *and you will know the truth, and the truth*
> *will make you free" (John 8:31-32, NASB).*

# I Want to Live Right, but I'm Still Hurting

One of the errors the church has made was to teach people that having faith means denying your feelings. However, balance is embracing my feelings while still believing in the LORD Jesus Christ is the fight many of us have. Jesus embraced his feelings when he was here on earth in bodily form; however, Christ never allowed his feelings to make him abort his purpose even when He felt like it.

> *"Then, accompanied by the disciples, Jesus left the upstairs room and went as usual to the Mount of Olives. There he told them, "Pray that you will not give in to temptation." He walked away, about a stone's throw, and knelt down and prayed, "Father, if you are willing, please take this cup of suffering away from me. Yet I want your will to be done, not mine." Then an angel from heaven appeared and strengthened him. He prayed more fervently, and he was in such agony of spirit that his sweat fell to the ground like great drops of blood. At last he stood up again and returned to the disciples, only to find them asleep, exhausted from grief. "Why are you sleeping?" he asked them. "Get up and pray, so that you will not give in to temptation"(Luke 22:35-46, NLT).*

> *"While Jesus was here on earth, he offered prayers and pleadings, with a loud cry and tears, to the one who could rescue him from*

*death. And God heard his prayers because of his deep reverence for God. Even though Jesus was God's Son, he learned obedience from the things he suffered"* (Hebrews 5:7-8, NLT).

*"So then, since we have a great High Priest who has entered heaven, Jesus the Son of God, let us hold firmly to what we believe. This High Priest of ours understands our weaknesses, for he faced all of the same testings we do, yet he did not sin. So let us come boldly to the throne of our gracious God. There we will receive his mercy, and we will find grace to help us when we need it most"* (Hebrews 4:14-16, NLT).

The greatest love story ever told was in the Bible. The love of Christ went deeper than Romeo or Juliet. They both ended up dying together. Christ died for us. It's not even a Bonnie and Clyde story. Christ was not a thief. He never died for someone else's spouse. Jesus Christ, the LORD God died for his bride (the Church). What amazes me is that Jesus Christ died for a church that did not always love Him, didn't always know Him, nor treated Him the way that we should have. He never took the church out on a date or tried to get to know us. Christ knew us before we were even born. He loved us with everlasting love.

Many are withholding the love they have for their significant other as a punishment until they break and cave in, doing what the withholding spouse wants them to do. However, Christ loves us knowing how difficult, moody, arrogant, and ungrateful we can be. Yet, the Bible made it clear that He decided to die. Nevertheless, there was a moment in the garden of Gethsemane where he felt the agony of what he wanted to do. **Real love does for us even when it hurts, but don't hurt the love that hurt Himself for us.**

Nevertheless, the above scriptures show us that the LORD Jesus Christ was tempted to give up His purpose in dying for his bride (the church) was due to the agony he felt. Christ is victorious, but He never allowed Himself to think like a victim. Jesus knew that his feeling was to be accepted as long as He rejected the temptation to seek revenge on the church after everything He has done for the church. Victorious people will be tempted to feel, and think, thoughts of revenge when they feel defeated. However, we remind ourselves that obedience to the will of God despite our sufferings is the key to coming out like pure gold.

> **Real love does for us even when it hurts, but don't hurt the love that hurt Himself for us.**

## "I'M NOT JESUS; I'M NOT THERE YET."

I can't speak for you, but I've been there. You might have read the previous paragraph and felt too hurt, angry, and frustrated to be like Jesus and accept your purpose because you're not being hurt, upset, angry, and tired of being nice to people who continuously take you for granted. However, you must have Christ's confidence within to know that whoever hurt you will never defeat you.

You see revenge is a time waster, and revenge seekers are not good with time management.

Revenge seekers are up at eight in the morning, on the phone gossiping about who they can't stand. Revenge seekers cannot enjoy what the LORD Jesus has done and is doing in their lives due to being upset with God for blessing their enemies. Yes, the revenge seeker is shocked that the LORD Jesus's mercy shines on the unjust as well as the just.

If we continue to succumb to the fantasy and temptation to get revenge, we will live and die miserably. Many of us refuse to move through the fear, hurt, pain, and frustration because of what we continuously say to ourselves about what has been done to us. We say things like:

- "I'm not going to move on until they apologize."
- "I'm not going to let that go until He leaves that other woman."
- "I'm not letting go of anything until I make them hurt like they made me hurt."
- "You don't know what they did to me."
- "I can't wait until I see them again."
- "Revenge is a dish best-served cold."

This negative self-talk will make the most beautiful personalities appear ugly. Marilyn Monroe said, "If you're going to be two-faced, make one of them pretty." You may be saying,

"How can I be two-faced when they are doing me wrong? I'm only doing to them what they did to me." Remember what I am about to say: **"The people who hurt us only win when we allow them to turn us into them."**

> **"The people who hurt us only win when we allow them to turn us into them."**

# Hurt on the Level I Trusted

Some people hurt us so that we might have even forgotten about it because we really didn't care about them in the first place. However, some people can hurt us so deeply that we just want to forget about all the pain, and leave town. King David put it this way:

> *"Fear and trembling grip me; horror has*
> *overwhelmed me.*
> *I said, "If only I had wings like a dove!*
> *I would fly away and find rest.*
> *How far away I would flee;*
> *I would stay in the wilderness. Selah*
> *I would hurry to my shelter*
> *from the raging wind and the storm."*
> *Lord, confuse and confound their speech,*
> *for I see violence and strife in the city;*
> *day and night they make the rounds on its*
> *walls.*
> *Crime and trouble are within it;*
> *destruction is inside it;*
> *oppression and deceit never*
> *leave its marketplace.*
> *Now it is not an enemy who insults me—*
> *otherwise, I could bear it;*
> *it is not a foe who rises up against me—*
> *otherwise, I could hide from him.*
> *But it is you, a man who is my peer,*
> *my companion and good friend!*

*We used to have close fellowship;*
*we walked with the crowd*
*into the house of God.*
*Let death take them by surprise;*
*let them go down to Sheol alive,*
*because evil is in their homes and within*
*them" (Psalms 55:5-15, CSB).*

David was so hurt by the betrayal that he wanted wings like a dove to fly away. It made it clear that this kind of pain and broken trust can never be accomplished by an enemy. You already know that your enemy does not like you. However, this kind of hurt can only come from trusted family members and friends. This is the kind of hurt and pain that makes us distrustful of the rest of the world, causing us to misjudge others before getting to know them.

David is so hurt that he is contemplating isolating himself. Are you allowing the hurt you went through to cause you to isolate yourself from others? If not careful, you might turn your back on the ones who the LORD Jesus could be used to propel you into your destiny. The Bible is so serious about these that the word of God cautions us to even be careful of how we treat strangers because some have been in the presence of angels unaware (Hebrews 13:2).

Wait a minute. Did you notice in the above passage that David was hurt by someone whom he use to attend church with? He is hurt by someone that he use to attend Church with. Let me pause and address those of you who are still suffering from church hurt. Yes, it is true that sometimes, many churches can be the coldest place on the block. Truth be told, many have left the church and refuse to return due to being hurt and devastated by those in the church they shared their secrets with.

However, when I go to a restaurant and have an issue with the food, or the waitress is being rude, leaving the restaurant isn't the first thing that comes to mind. The first thing I want to do is talk to the manager. The Bible made it clear that the LORD Jesus Christ is the head of the Church (Ephesians 5:23). Why leave the church when you can speak to the head of the church who is Christ Jesus the LORD?

Furthermore, we leave the church when we are hurt, offended, and upset, but what if we talked about how we hurt the head of the church, the LORD Jesus Christ? We didn't always pray to the LORD Jesus the way that we should have. We have taken the LORD Jesus for granted at times.
We have even backslid after being saved (let us be clear you don't have to leave the church to backslide). What if the LORD banned us from the church because of our past sins and current faults?

Additionally, notice another thing. David was so hurt by the betrayal that David prays for harm to happen to them. Listen to me, regardless of how much someone has done to you- never pray for bad things to happen. Now you might say, "If David did it, I can too. It's in the Bible." No. David was hurt. We can go to heaven with a hurting heart, but we cannot go to heaven with a hating heart.

In fact, the LORD Jesus Christ corrected David's prayer:

> *"But to you who are willing to listen, I say, love your enemies! Do good to those who hate you. Bless those who curse you. Pray for those who hurt you. If someone slaps you on one cheek, offer the other cheek also. If someone demands*

*your coat, offer your shirt also. Give to anyone who asks; and when things are taken away from you, don't try to get them back. Do to others as you would like them to do to you"* (Luke 6:27-29, NLT).

I will leave this with you, on the topic of church hurt, when the church hurt Jesus, he said,

*"Father, forgive them; for they know not what they do"* (Luke 23:34, KJV).

## "I Trust You to Be Who You Say You're Going to Be"

One of the most interesting things about Joseph's story, as many times as I have heard it, Joseph never trusted his brothers again. He still loves them but acts like he doesn't trust them. Joseph is hurt, but not stupid. He saw with his own eyes how ruthless his brothers could be. Although his heart may no longer trust them, he still loves them.

In the 1996 film, *A Thin Line Between Love & Hate*, Mia, played by Regina King, and Darnell, played by Martin Lawrence get into a conversation. Martin asks Mia, "Do you trust me?" Well, after pausing for a few seconds, she stated, "I trust you to be who you're going to be." That one line never left my head. Many of us are stressed out because we

> we only have a hard time being in the same room with people we don't trust when we haven't accepted them for who they are.

think we cannot be under the same rule as people we cannot trust. However, **we only have a hard time being in the same room with people we don't trust when we haven't accepted them for who they are.**

## You Don't Remember Me Do You?

*"When Jacob heard that grain was available in Egypt, he said to his sons, "Why are you standing around looking at one another? I have heard there is grain in Egypt. Go down there and buy enough grain to keep us alive. Otherwise, we'll die." So Joseph's ten older brothers went down to Egypt to buy grain. But Jacob wouldn't let Joseph's younger brother, Benjamin, go with them, for fear some harm might come to him. So Jacob's sons arrived in Egypt along with others to buy food, for the famine was in Canaan as well. Since Joseph was governor of all Egypt and in charge of selling grain to all the people, it was to him that his brothers came. When they arrived, they bowed before him with their faces to the ground. Joseph recognized his brothers instantly, but he pretended to be a stranger and spoke harshly to them. "Where are you from?" he demanded. "From the land of Canaan," they replied. "We have come to buy food." Although Joseph recognized his brothers, they didn't recognize him" (Genesis 42:1-8, NLT).*

One thing about those tables, they turn, don't they? Let me explain the above passage. Joseph is rich, in a place of power, and his dreams are coming true. His brothers are all broke and living in a famine. They hear that there is food in Egypt and decide to go get some. They don't realize that the one who has the power to help them get food is standing in front of them, and that is their brother, Joseph- whom they thought was long gone by now. Therefore, the real question is not why is Joseph alive, but why are his brothers alive.

Sometimes God will let your enemies live just as long as you to show you that their words did not have the last say over your life. God will allow the child molester to live to see you prosper. God will allow the people who left you for dead life to watch you leave the place they left you in but had spies watching in their absence. Most importantly, God lets you live to show your enemies that Jesus Christ is still God!

Before, he was just Joseph, their brother. Then they leave him as Joseph the slave. Now they will soon learn that this is Joseph the governor. I heard God tell Abraham, "I will make your name great" (Genesis 12:2). Now don't get this twisted: God is not doing this so that you can brag and show off out of hurt, anger, and bitterness. God allows us to rise out of the ashes of the furnace our enemies have placed us in to show them that he is in control. Yes, they meet again, but only the victorious Joseph recognized the defeated brothers who sold him into slavery.

Some people will not remember what they did to you, and that can be frustrating when you spent years living with the adrenaline rush of seeing them suffer like or more than they have made you. Here me good when I tell you the enemy is using the pain that you have endured against you. Joseph was not about to go out like that. He couldn't help what they did, but Joseph remembered what the LORD had done for him.

## NEGLECTING PEOPLE WHO NEVER DID ANYTHING TO YOU

There is nothing as bad as having someone make you pay for what someone else did to you. One of the things I have noticed about the life of Joseph is that he is good at not allowing others to pay for what his brothers did to him. Although this takes a lot of practice, Joseph had a lot of God. **When we give into the temptation to get revenge, the people who remained loyal to us end up suffering.** There are only two primary reasons why we make others pay for what someone else did to us that I will share with you now.

> **When we give into the temptation to get revenge, the people who remained loyal to us end up suffering.**

1.   We aren't healed

Evil people don't always hurt people; hurt people hurt people. Our expectations are hurt. Our trust is broken. Our dreams are tarnished. Our secrets were exposed. We are afraid, angry, and frustrated, and don't feel like hearing "turn the other cheek," or "what would Jesus do?" This heart of ours is searching for answers, closure, and comfort.

One of the best things that we can do for the people who came into our lives is to give them a healed or healing version of ourselves.

2.    We refuse to forgive

Notice I did not say that we cannot forgive. We refuse to forgive. This is a pity party at its best. The Bible, however, had another way of phrasing it: "Refused to be comforted."

> "Judah said to his brothers, "What do we gain if we kill our brother and cover up his blood? Come on, let's sell him to the Ishmaelites and not lay a hand on him, for he is our brother, our own flesh," and his brothers agreed. When Midianite traders passed by, his brothers pulled Joseph out of the pit and sold him for twenty pieces of silver to the Ishmaelites, who took Joseph to Egypt. When Reuben returned to the pit and saw that Joseph was not there, he tore his clothes. He went back to his brothers and said, "The boy is gone! What am I going to do?" So they took Joseph's robe, slaughtered a male goat, and dipped the robe in its blood. They sent the long-sleeved robe to their father and said, "We found this. Examine it. Is it your son's robe or not?" His father recognized it. "It is my son's robe," he said. "A vicious animal has devoured him. Joseph has been torn to pieces!" Then Jacob tore his clothes, put sackcloth around his waist, and mourned for his son many days. All his sons and daughters tried to comfort him, but he refused to be comforted. "No," he said. "I will go down to Sheol to my

*son, mourning." And his father wept for him. Meanwhile, the Midianites sold Joseph in Egypt to Potiphar, an officer of Pharaoh and the captain of the guards" (Genesis 37:26-36, CSB).*

Now let's talk about Joseph's father. Jacob loved Joseph very much to the degree his brothers thought he was Jacob's favorite. They envied him because of the coat his father gave him. They also envied him because of the dreams that he had. Even Joseph's father felt some kind of way himself. Nevertheless, when his brothers made up a lie, in the above passage, about his death, Jacob is so hurt that he refuses to be comforted. He simply wanted to be left alone.

While Jacobs's grief can be understood, **many of us are grieving what we refuse to forgive.** The LORD Jesus Christ has given us many opportunities to move forward; however, in our wilful pride, we refused to move through our pain out of fear of being hurt again. **One thing I can promise is that seeking revenge will get us hurt again.** As Dr. Iona Locke put it, "You can't sin successfully."

> **many of us are grieving what we refuse to forgive.**

> **One thing I can promise is that seeking revenge will get us hurt again.**

## What Does the Temptation to seek Revenge Have to do with my Destiny?

It makes you lose faith in who is in charge. This temptation to get even makes you plot to hurt who God used to bless you. Giving into the temptation to get even is a perception issue that we have that causes us to maximize the identity of the perpetrator rather than keep our integrity, focusing on the Creator. No one who hurt us is worth us losing our destiny over. I mean no one! If we really want to know how much faith we are walking in we would just have to look at where we are in letting God fight our battles of heartbreak.

# The Temptation to Live on Memory Lane

"This one thing I do; forgetting those
things which are behind; reaching to
those things are before." -Philippians 3:13

Christ has gifted me with an unusual, good memory. The only problem with that is that my flesh doesn't want to forget what my spirit wants to forgive. Truth be told forgiveness is hard when you have a great memory, especially when you remember how good you were to them simultaneously. When you spent money did not have to help them when they had nothing. You don't mind seeing them get on their feet. The only thing that is frustrating is that they did not even say thank you.

However, Joseph's story has a slightly different narrative. Joseph's brothers are not the ones who get on their feet; Joseph is. Joseph is in such a place of power (that can only come from the LORD Jesus Christ, God Almighty Himself) that he can destroy his brothers if he wanted to. Nevertheless, that is not what Joseph wants. He does not want to get even, but the memories just won't stop.

## Some Things You Bury Alive Don't Die

The technology of today makes it hard to bury what you want to die quietly. In a world where exes stalk your Facebook page, family members drive past you without blowing or waving and following you through a fake page on Instagram, and enemies comment underneath your news feed just to make you their friend (not knowing you know what they're up to but just playing along) - makes moving on a little more strenuous.

Let's not forget, even if you don't have social media or don't even care to know who is watching your Facebook page, some people won't let things die. They will always remind you of the events, memories, and sad truths you want to forget. However, what do you do when you're the one that is trying to bury something alive that is not a grudge, but your loving heart?

## When My Heart Attacks

Have you ever hated yourself for loving the wrong person? Have you ever been angry with yourself for crying over those who told you to move on with a calm smile on their face? Have you been frustrated and hard on yourself because forcing yourself to move on as fast as your friends and family do isn't working? This is what I call "My heart attacks." What do I mean?

The heart attacks I'm referring to are more than a sudden and sometimes fatal occurrence of coronary thrombosis, resulting in the death of a heart muscle. The kind of heart attack I am referring to is the heart attack that comes from having a pure heart that only God can give that sometimes makes you care more than you wished. Yes, many who say they don't care really do. They just don't want to because it hurts to care, especially when you care for the ones who don't care to apologize for breaking your heart.

Truth be told, it hurts to care. Joseph had a loving heart. That's just who he is. That is the way that the LORD Jesus created him. He does not hate his brothers. If there were telephones back then, he probably would have tried to call them. If there were phones, he might have tried to text them. Nevertheless, Joseph is learning to accept what he could not change. Joseph is about to create new memories

## MAKING NEW MEMORIES

*"Although Joseph recognized his brothers, they didn't recognize him. And he remembered the dreams he'd had about them many years before. He said to them, "You are spies! You have come to see how vulnerable our land has become." "No, my lord!" they exclaimed. "Your servants have simply come to buy food. We are all brothers—members of the same family. We are honest men, sir! We are not spies!" "Yes, you are!" Joseph insisted. "You have come to see how vulnerable our land has become." "Sir," they said, "there are actually twelve of us. We, your servants, are all brothers, sons of a man living in the land of Canaan. Our youngest brother is back*

*there with our father right now, and one of our brothers is no longer with us." But Joseph insisted, "As I said, you are spies! This is how I will test your story. I swear by the life of Pharaoh that you will never leave Egypt unless your youngest brother comes here! One of you must go and get your brother. I'll keep the rest of you here in prison. Then we'll find out whether or not your story is true. By the life of Pharaoh, if it turns out that you don't have a younger brother, then I'll know you are spies"* (Genesis 42:8-16, NLT).

Joseph's brother is in a position that might have surprised them but only became a confirmation to "the dreamer." Joseph tried to tell them, but they did not listen. He pleaded, but they were too jealous to listen. He finally has a chance to get even. Additionally, what makes this juicy is that they are asking for help. Joseph is in the right position to say no. Joseph wants to help them, but he takes a moment to cry.

## PRIVATE TEARS

Sometimes people don't understand you when you had to teach yourself how to be strong because of what you endured. Some of us wear our pain so well that people envy our strength-not realizing that we are all over the place inside. We had to teach ourselves how to keep smiling while hurting inside on the job. We taught ourselves how to be guarded so that no one will ever hurt us again. Some of us have become so guarded that we have become "difficult."

However, Joseph's strength did not come from being guarded. Joseph's strength comes from the LORD Jesus Christ. Joseph's strength stems from the fact that God never left him when his brothers left. In fact, The LORD Jesus Christ, God Almighty, was there all the time. Many of us are the recipients of God's presence in our lives. If we had not had a relationship with the LORD Jesus Christ, we would have lost our minds a long time ago. Nevertheless, you can have Christ in your life and still have heartbreak in your life. Joseph was good at being strong until he sees his brothers again.

Joseph looks at his brothers and has a flashback of the dream that he told his brothers. Also, with those members came tears. Joseph tears. His brothers, on the other hand, do not recognize him, but they had a flashback of their own.

> *"So Joseph put them all in prison for three days. On the third day Joseph said to them, "I am a God-fearing man. If you do as I say, you will live. If you really are honest men, choose one of your brothers to remain in prison. The rest of you may go home with grain for your starving families. But you must bring your youngest brother back to me. This will prove that you are telling the truth, and you will not die." To this they agreed. Speaking among themselves, they said, "Clearly we are being punished because of what we did to Joseph long ago. We saw his anguish when he pleaded for his life, but we wouldn't listen. That's why we're in this trouble." "Didn't I tell you not to sin against the boy?" Reuben asked. "But you*

*wouldn't listen. And now we have to answer for his blood!" Of course, they didn't know that Joseph understood them, for he had been speaking to them through an interpreter. Now he turned away from them and began to weep. When he regained his composure, he spoke to them again. Then he chose Simeon from among them and had him tied up right before their eyes"* (Genesis 42:17-24, NLT).

Joseph remembers from a perspective that his brothers don't recall. Joseph's tears come from heartbreak while his brothers' words reveal a guilty conscience. They meet again, all in the same room, but each narrative was different. A daughter, who finally meets her dad, she was upset for never wanting her. All she remembers was that her mom has told her how much her father beat her. The father, on the other hand, tells her that all he remembers is coming home on his lunch break and finding her mom with another man. Or take the wife who sees a whole different view of what she remembers.

When the daughter finally confronts her mother about her father's version of the narrative. The mother erupts in anger. She questions her daughter for not trusting her enough and going to talk to her father after everything that she has done for her. The mother is already coming off as guilty, being defensive, and making her daughter feel like she betrayed her mother for wanting to have a conversation with her father. Evidently, the original version that the mother gave her daughter was not the truth. It was her version due to wanting to sleep with and be with her husband's brother, who is her daughter's uncle.

You see the rapist has a different perspective. The victim remembers from a different perspective, and the one in the middle of the drama, like Joseph, has a different memory. You see each person's memory is predicated on their perspective. Allow me to take time to elaborate on what I mean as we delve into each person's memory in the story.

- **Joseph's Brothers- Memories of Guilt–** The brothers of Joseph are in no place to handle the guilt of what they have done to their brother. **No one hates being confronted like someone who never expected to get caught.** Keep in mind they thought they would never see Joseph again. When people have a guilty conscience, they avoid you. When people have a guilty conscience, they talk around certain questions without answering them directly. Real guilt will catch a ride to work with you on a good morning. Real guilt will make you depressed. Real guilt will make you stay with someone you're not in love with only because you both have a child together. Memories of guilt will also make us think that we are not forgiven. You see, it's one thing to have guilt about what you haven't confessed. However, it is another thing to have guilt after you have admitted the wrong you've done. Memories of guilt are a temptation to the individual that the LORD Jesus has already forgiven. Many of us who have already asked for Christ's forgiveness have a hard time accepting His forgiveness because we have a hard time trusting in Christ's forgiveness.

- **Reuben- Memories of Not Standing Up for the Ones You Love-** We see this one happen all the time. Reuben represents all of us who don't think we were in the wrong because we did not pull the trigger. We didn't start the gossip. You will notice of all of Joseph's brothers, Reuben is the only brother in the story who, although hated Joseph, did not want to see him die in the prison. Now is a good time to remind you that just because your enemy doesn't want you to die doesn't mean they have a change of heart. Some people just want us to stay alive so that we can stay with them and can continue to use us. Nevertheless, we have to forgive ourselves for not taking action when we should have. Reuben did not realize that he was a part of God's plan for Joseph.

- **Jacob- Memories of surprise** – This one may hurt the most. Jacob never planned on burying his children, especially Joseph. As quiet as it's kept, Joseph was Jacobs's favorite son. He was such a favorite that Joseph gave him a coat of many colors. Jacobs's memories were memories that he did not want to have. It's hard to lose a person that we put a lot of trust in, especially when we know that they cannot be replaced. Jacob's temptation, like many of us who lost someone that we feel, cannot be replaced, is to develop a co-dependency with anyone that comes close, which is Jacob's next youngest son- Benjamin.

- **Joseph- Mixed Memories-** Joseph's memories are memories of confusion. Memories where the best of times and the worst of times collide. Joseph has more memories of his brothers hating them than he does of them loving him. In fact, the Bible says nothing about how his brothers treated him before his dream. Nevertheless, we have more information than we need on how much jealousy and hatred can make the good days questionable. **It's hard to trust someone who secretly wants your life.** However, the brothers of Joseph have gone beyond keeping their jealousy a secret. They made it known in their actions, plots, and abandonment of their brother.

> It's hard to trust someone who secretly wants your life.

## Memories I Wish I Had

By the same token, some of us are not traumatized by a father who abused us; we are traumatized by memories of fantasies of having an imaginary father come to our school games. The little girl is not crying over a father that molested her but wishes she had a dad that would hug her. Some of us watch families on Facebook, only wishing that our family could get along in that way. Oh yes! It is possible to be traumatized by what never happened.

Maybe Joseph wished he had memories of his brothers celebrating his dreams. Nevertheless, all Joseph has is the memories of what did happen. Yes, have you ever said to yourself and thought about what happened? Have you ever said to yourself, "He really did molest me," "She really just said that to me," "No child should have never had to go through that," or "I didn't see that coming."

Or have you thought to yourself, "I wish my father was around," "I wish I had a man that would not cheat on me," or "I wish that I could stop wishing?" These thoughts can make us so depressed that we refuse to be comforted. These thoughts will make us forget that "the last shall be first and the first shall be last" (Matthew 20:16).

## THE CONFRONTATION

I wonder if Joseph ever believed he would see his brothers again. The Bible does not tell us. What we do know, based on the holy scriptures, is that when Joseph sees his brothers again, he is not quick to reveal himself or confront them about what they did to him. He instantly recognizes them after they bow down to him (Genesis 42:6-8). There are a few things that Joseph does to his brothers that, from a psychological and therapeutic perspective are not healthy in our dealing with people we meet again who left a bad memory/memories in the reservoirs of our mind.

1. **Tone is Important**- The Bible makes it clear that Joseph speaks "roughly" to his brothers (Genesis 42:7) when he recognized them. Often when we have hurt others in the past, their demeanor, tone, and body language can come off sarcastic, mean, and out of the left field.

   They never told us how they really felt, but now they have been holding it in for so long that their sarcasm is obviously noticeable, but the root of the problem is still covered up. The Bible is clear that *"A gentle answer deflects anger, but harsh words make tempers flare" (Proverbs 15:1, NLT).* **Before confronting the ones, who hurt us, it is pivotal that we first confront ourselves.** We have to make sure that we do it from a confidence rooted in Christ, humility, and from a healed mind. Joseph was done wrong, but that gave no excuse for his tone to be rough toward his brothers. "Be ye angry, and sin not" (Ephesians 4:26).

2.  **Passive Aggressive**- Yes, you read correctly. Joseph became passive-aggressive.

    In an endeavor to make sure that his father and youngest brother are alive, he sends his brothers back home, placing money in their sack to see if they really have changed their character for the better. This is a good time to pause and say that **everyone we confront will not change**. So, we must remember to keep our trust in the LORD Jesus and not in the one we are confronting.

3.  **Keeps the Game Face on**- Joseph does not want them to know that he recognizes them. However, he can hear his brothers talking through an interpreter (Genesis 42:22-23). There can be a myriad of reasons why Joseph is not ready to reveal himself to his brothers. The "game face" is an African American

colloquialism, which means that we are hiding how we truly feel so we don't appear weak or vulnerable.

Many of us have kept the game face on for so long to the degree to which it has become too heavy of a burden to bear. It's so easy for us to get married with the game face on; remain in therapy with the game face on; even go to church with the game face on. Aren't you tired of being hidden in plain sight?

## Bringing Up What You Said You Forgave

Listen, if I don't love the LORD Jesus Christ for anything else, I love Him for forgiving me! I'm thankful that I repented of my sins, was baptized in the NAME of the LORD Jesus Christ, and filled with the Holy Spirit, according to Acts 2:38. I take Christ's forgiveness very personally because he did not have to forgive me, but He did. He chose us from the foundation of the world (Romans 8:29).

What I am also glad about the forgiveness of Jesus Christ is that He does not forgive the way humans do. **No one brings up what they said in the past like people who said all is forgiven.** No one wants to continue to live with, be married to, or have friendships where their wrongs from the past are constantly coming up. What adds insult to injury is when it is brought up out of sarcasm, passive-aggressiveness, or to make the individual feel just as bad as they made us feel.

If you aren't over it yet, just say that. It's better than lying and pretending that it's all good. However, what you cannot do is allow that anger to rent property in your body. If you are already filled with the holy spirit, your body is the temple of the holy spirit (1 Corinthians 6:19-20).

If someone has apologized to us for the hurt they have caused us, and they have apologized in sincerity, then our refusal to forgive them is an internal issue. The word of God puts it this way, *"Keep thy heart with all diligence; for out of it are the issues of life" (Proverbs 4:23, KJV)*. What place in your memory does the current pain they caused you took you back to? Did what happened to make you feel unloved, insecure, or doubting your worth? Normally when we refuse to accept a sincere, heartfelt, apology- it's because it has taken us back to an insecure place, and insecure beliefs about ourselves that we worked so hard to keep suppressed.

## REMEMBERING WHO FORGOT YOU SO FAST

Have you ever tried to forget who forgot you? I mean they proved they forgot you. They post happy selfies on social media and forget you. I mean moved on and get married and forget you. I mean blocked you off social media and forget you. I mean seeing you in public and kept driving to forget you. I'm talking about seeing them hang with people they use to talk about with you and forget you. Joseph had to face a season of being forgotten when he asked to be remembered.

*"And Joseph said to him, "This is the interpretation of it: The three branches are three days. Now within three days Pharaoh*

*will lift up your head and restore you to your place, and you will put Pharaoh's cup in his hand according to the former manner, when you were his butler.* **But remember me when it is well with you, and please show kindness to me; make mention of me to Pharaoh, and get me out of this house.** *For indeed I was stolen away from the land of the Hebrews; and also I have done nothing here that they should put me into the dungeon." When the chief baker saw that the interpretation was good, he said to Joseph, "I also was in my dream, and there were three white baskets on my head. In the uppermost basket were all kinds of baked goods for Pharaoh, and the birds ate them out of the basket on my head." So Joseph answered and said, "This is the interpretation of it: The three baskets are three days. Within three days Pharaoh will lift off your head from you and hang you on a tree, and the birds will eat your flesh from you." Now it came to pass on the third day, which was Pharaoh's birthday, that he made a feast for all his servants; and he lifted up the head of the chief butler and of the chief baker among his servants. Then he restored the chief butler to his butlership again, and he placed the cup in Pharaoh's hand. But he hanged the chief baker, as Joseph had interpreted to them.* **Yet the chief butler did not remember Joseph but forgot him"** (Genesis 40:12-23, NKJV).

Joseph was so gifted that his gift helped another prisoner get out of jail. He was so confident in his God-given gift to interpret dreams that he asks the chief butler not to forget him. Nevertheless, he gets out and forgets about Joseph. What do you do when you've been forgotten by people who you know have the power to help you? What makes matters worse is when you remind them not to forget you. **I need to pause right now and tell someone by divine inspiration not to remind someone to not forget you.**

> **I need to pause right now and tell someone by divine inspiration not to remind someone to not forget you.**

One thing Joseph had not realized is that God did not just bless him with favor;

God also blessed him with an appointed time. This is the frustration of having the favor of God in our lives. As gifted as you are, you don't have the money yet to get your dream off the ground. As anointed as you are, you feel like everyone else's ministry is growing except yours. Joseph was forgotten on purpose because it was not God's timing for the king of Egypt to remember him; nevertheless, Christ never forgot him.

*"Then it came to pass, at the end of two full years, that Pharaoh had a dream; and behold, he stood by the river. Suddenly there came up out of the river seven cows, fine looking and fat; and they fed in the meadow. Then behold,*

seven other cows came up after them out of the river, ugly and gaunt, and stood by the other cows on the bank of the river. And the ugly and gaunt cows ate up the seven fine looking and fat cows. So Pharaoh awoke. He slept and dreamed a second time; and suddenly seven heads of grain came up on one stalk, plump and good. Then behold, seven thin heads, blighted by the east wind, sprang up after them. And the seven thin heads devoured the seven plump and full heads. So Pharaoh awoke, and indeed, it was a dream. Now it came to pass in the morning that his spirit was troubled, and he sent and called for all the magicians of Egypt and all its wise men. And Pharaoh told them his dreams, but there was no one who could interpret them for Pharaoh. Then the chief butler spoke to Pharaoh, saying: "I remember my faults this day. When Pharaoh was angry with his servants, and put me in custody in the house of the captain of the guard, both me and the chief baker, we each had a dream in one night, he and I. Each of us dreamed according to the interpretation of his own dream. Now there was a young Hebrew man with us there, a servant of the captain of the guard. And we told him, and he interpreted our dreams for us; to each man he interpreted according to his own dream. And it came to pass, just as he interpreted for us, so it happened. He restored me to my office, and he hanged him." Then Pharaoh sent and called Joseph, and they brought him quickly out of the dungeon; and *he shaved, changed his clothing, and came to Pharaoh. And Pharaoh said to Joseph, "I have had a dream, and there is no one who can interpret it. But I have heard it said of you that you can understand a dream, to interpret it." So Joseph answered Pharaoh, saying, "It is not in me; God will give Pharaoh an answer of peace" (Genesis 41:1-16, NKJV).*

Well, as we say in church, "Look at God!" The LORD Jesus allowed Joseph to be remembered by the chief butler at the right time. You've got to trust God's timing when you're tempted to live on memory lane. No good thing does God withhold from those who walk upright before Him, according to Psalms 84:10. The devil wants you to think that because someone has forgotten about you for a season, you'll never get back up on your feet, but that devil is a liar!

## A Lesson on the Temptation of Living in the Memories of Our Past Sins

This is something that many of us know too well. Nothing can haunt you like memories of our past sins. I'm talking about sins that could end your career. Sins that can end your marriage. Secret sins that, although you've asked Christ for forgiveness, those memories show up unannounced at the house of your heart and get past the security of your soul, refusing to leave the reservoirs of your mind. The devil knows he cannot kill the anointing on our lives but his next best effort is to keep you in a mental and emotional prison of solitary confinement. Talk to anyone who comes from a negative background and made mistakes that almost ruined their reputation, and they will tell you that they had or continue to fight the enemy's accusations against them of what Christ has already forgiven. By the way, don't you know when the LORD Jesus Christ (God Almighty) forgives you as if you never sinned? The devil loves to bring up what Christ has already forgiven you of.

## WHAT DOES THE TEMPTATION TO LIVE ON MEMORY LANE HAVE TO DO WITH MY DESTINY?

We are often stuck on memory lane when we maximize the hurt and pain, or think that the good times are the only good times that we will have. Memory lane is when your faith is in the good old days while your discouragement is in the days ahead. Real faith knows that there is no way that Christ would take something from me without giving something to me. Real faith knows that sooner or later, God will work in our favor, Real faith knows that as long as Christ is with me, I haven't seen my best days yet.

# The Temptation to be Petty

"...by the way, I'm petty." -Anonymous

We have all heard the saying, "Nobody is perfect but God." There are quite a few words in the Bible that many have a problem with. One of those words is "perfect". We have a hard accepting this word for a plethora of reasons. One of the reasons we have an issue with the word perfect, for one, is due to our own guilt and struggle with trying to fight the fleshly desires that war against our soul. When we continuously give in to the same secret sins that we just repented of yesterday, we gave up on trusting the Holy Spirit to guide us through our habitual temptations.

Another reason why we have a problem with the word perfect is due to our lack of faith in God's word concerning who He says we are and can be. *"Be ye therefore perfect, even as your Father which is in heaven is perfect"* (Matthew 5:48, KJV). Many of us look at the word perfect from the English language definition, which means completely free from faults or defects.

However, the Bible's original language was written in Hebrew (Old Testament), and Greek (new testament).

The new testament word for perfect in Matthew 5:48 is *teleios,* which means to be complete, fulfillment. What does that mean according to the word of God? The Apostle Paul reminds the baptized believers that we are complete in Christ Jesus (Colossians 2:10). So when Jesus said, *"Be ye therefore perfect, even as your Father which is in heaven is perfect"* (*Matthew 5:48, KJV),* He is saying to be complete and fulfilled in Him. I don't know how you see it, but according to the word of God, I don't know anyone who can fulfill me and complete me like the LORD Jesus Christ. Jesus Christ is the only one who can complete us for the LORD Jesus Christ is God Almighty Himself.

What makes a beautiful, intelligent woman stay with a man that perpetually uses her as a punching bag? What makes a good man stay with a woman that verbally abuses him in private and ultimately in public? What makes others stay in a dead job when they have been offered an ample amount of opportunities to have the career that the LORD Jesus Christ has for them? The only answer besides fear is the irrational mindset of thinking that person or job completes and fulfills them. Some people have been left, cheated on, and used by a narcissist, but in their own self-doubt, insecurities, and lack of Christ's Confidence, still want closure from that individual. Why? The person has mentally, emotionally, and even physically abused them to the degree to which they believe they are nothing at all without that person.

Nevertheless, the Bible makes it clear that our wholeness can only come from the LORD Jesus Christ, who is God Almighty. Trying to make that abuser answer the phone will only lead to more heartbreak. Trusting a liar, who lied throughout the whole relationship, to give you closure will only result in more lies. Trying to make certain people you love be to you what they cannot be to you will lead to more insecurities and agitation. Consequently, you will be drained. Why don't you just come to Jesus for closure? Why don't you just come to Jesus for not only does He has answers; Christ is the answer!

## From Maturity to Pettiness

Thirdly, we have a problem with the word perfect because we are not through being petty. According to the oxford dictionary, petty is defined as small and unimportant. Read that slowly. The question is how do we get Joseph to see that what his brothers did to him was small and important? How do you tell someone who was cheated on and got an STI (sexually transmitted infection) that the person who cheated was just petty? How do you tell the father that wants to be a good daddy that his "baby mommy" holding custody is unimportant and a small matter? How do you tell the employee who trained the person who blackmailed them that it is a small and unimportant matter?

To understand the injustices that were done to us without explanation, we must be spiritually minded. The Bible makes it clear that our intellectual fleshly mind cannot comprehend the purpose of the LORD Jesus Christ for our lives.

> *"Yet among the mature we do impart wisdom, although it is not a wisdom of this age or of the rulers of this age, who are doomed to pass away. But we impart a secret and hidden*

*wisdom of God, which God decreed before the ages for our glory. None of the rulers of this age understood this, for if they had, they would not have crucified the Lord of glory. But, as it is written, "What no eye has seen, nor ear heard, nor the heart of man imagined, what God has prepared for those who love him"— these things God has revealed to us through the Spirit. For the Spirit searches everything, even the depths of God. For who knows a person's thoughts except the spirit of that person, which is in him? So also no one comprehends the thoughts of God except the Spirit of God. Now we have received not the spirit of the world, but the Spirit who is from God, that we might understand the things freely given us by God. And we impart this in words not taught by human wisdom but taught by the Spirit, interpreting spiritual truths to those who are spiritual. The natural person does not accept the things of the Spirit of God, for they are folly to him, and he is not able to understand them because they are spiritually discerned. The spiritual person judges all things, but is himself to be judged by no one. "For who has understood the mind of the Lord so as to instruct him?" But we have the mind of Christ" (1 Corinthians 2:6-16).*

Notice the above massage begins with the word mature in verse six. The word of God reminds us that the people of the body of Christ have a hidden that one cannot matriculate from Yale, Harvard, or Morehouse. You need the gift of the Holy

Ghost to get the hidden wisdom of God. This kind of wisdom is what the above passages declare that rulers of this age did not have because if they did, they would have never tried to put Jesus Christ on the cross. This wisdom that the Apostle Paul talked about is not a new revelation; this wisdom simply explains the scriptures as it relates to our experiences.

Joseph had no Bible, for the Bible was not written yet. Joseph had God. Still, that was good enough because Jesus is a God of His word, for Jesus is the word of God (John 1:1). Now let's be honest, **it's hard to act mature when we don't know what God has for us on the other side of the pain.** Joseph did not know that he would be the Governor of Egypt. He did not know that all things were working together for the good. He did not know that the temptations on the side of his hurt could not be compared to the blessing that was on the other side.

## I Don't Have Answers, but I Have Faith in God

What do you do when God is taking you to a palace of blessing, but he chooses to take you through the route of the valley of the shadow of death? What do you do when God has a place that you can call your own but you have a hard time embracing it after being abandoned by your own? What do you do when God is not through with you, but He has you placed in a family that is through with you? Joseph had no insight on this at first, but he had integrity. His integrity stemmed from his faith in God.

You need faith when the love of your life sleeps with your sister. You need faith when family walks away. You need faith when children stand in your face and curse you out like you are one of the fellas of the street. You need faith when you trusted someone with your credit card and you have no money when you go to the ATM. I'm not talking about Sunday morning faith. I'm not referring to praise breaking faith. I'm talking about the kind of faith that helps you to walk in the consistency of integrity. I am talking about faith that keeps you or stops you from being petty.

If Joseph had gone to a psychologist, he might have been diagnosed with PTSD or trauma-related mental illness. The brother had dreams but was living a nightmare. Betrayal will make some of the most gifted, talented, and kind-hearted individuals become cynical, bitter, angry, and downright petty. Joseph has a moment of pettiness where he places money in their sack to test their loyalty.

## Never Give Satan Something to Use Against You

Now let's be fair and clear: I could see why Joseph is moving the way that he moves with his brothers; however, placing money in their sack to set them up was uncalled for. Joseph was testing their loyalty, but he may still be wishing for his brothers to be who they are not right now. **Many of us have had moments where we came outside of who we are to go inside someone else looking for what they did not have to give.**

they are not right now. **Many of us have had moments where**

**we came outside of who we are to go inside someone else looking for what they did not have to give.**

The word of God teaches us that prolonged anger gives "place" to the devil (Ephesians 4:26- 27). Many times when we do petty things that we have never done before we have reached a place of pain that we have never been through before or is tired of experiencing. Here me real good when I tell you that we are all entitled to a breaking point in our lives. It is even possible to break at the breaking point.

However, what Christ has never wanted us to do was give room to pettiness at our breaking point. God doesn't want you to slash his tires when you find receipts in your husbands' pockets of him taking another woman out for dinner. God doesn't want you to sleep with your sister's man to get back at her for sleeping with your boyfriend in high school. **That grudge you're holding is giving Satan something to use against you.** What do I mean? Jesus Christ makes it clear that our prayers will not be answered and that we won't be forgiven when we harbor resentment toward someone else.

> **That grudge you're holding is giving Satan something to use against you.**

Satan is a mastermind. He will give you a good idea (which cannot be God's idea) to use against us later. He will give you an idea to sleep around because your wife is using sex as a weapon. Next, he will use that to kill your ministry when the screenshots come out to expose you. Satan will give you an idea to start a church when God has not released you yet because He still wants you to serve your current Pastor. Consequently, your ministry will decline because you refused to trust God to make you ruler over much after being faithful over a few.

On the contrary, you may be feeling like you have heard the right message at the wrong time. You may be feeling like it's too late because you already gave the enemy too much territory. Nevertheless, I have good news for you! Although satan may be the accuser of the brethren, the Bible made it clear that Jesus Christ is our advocate (1 John 2:1-2). You may have allowed the devil room in your life, but the Holy Ghost has the power to give him an eviction notice.

The LORD Jesus Christ is calling you out of that dark place of resentment and rage to trust Him with your hurt and pain. He is calling you to lean on his word regarding the pain from your past.

## WHAT DOES THE TEMPTATION TO BE PETTY HAVE TO DO WITH MY DESTINY?

At the time of Joseph's act of pettiness, he was already in the place of blessing. He was already the prince of Egypt. At the age of thirty, God had him established. No weapon formed against Joseph was able to prosper. Joseph knew that God was the one that brought him to this place of blessing. However, at that moment, Joseph acted like he did not already have victory.

The Bible makes it clear that "In all these things we are more than conquerors through Him that loved us (Romans 8:37, NKJV). However, Joseph's blessing did not start in the palace. The Bible said that God gave Joseph favor in prison (Genesis 39:21). Joseph had a testimony that God was there all the time. Before you allow the temptation to be petty to ruin your future and cause unnecessary consequences, take a moment and remind your- self of everything that the LORD Jesus Christ has brought you through despite the betrayal that you've faced.

Remind yourself that Jesus Christ didn't let depression take you out after that rape. Remind yourself how the LORD Jesus did not allow what your family predicated on you to come to pass. Remind yourself of how your third-grade teacher's prediction that you would amount to nothing was a lie from the pit of hell. Remind yourself that God's word had and still has the final say over your life.

I don't know how hurt you are, but God does. He knows about the abandonment. He knows about the rape. He knows about the lies and rumors. He knows about the pain and rejection. He knows about the injustice done to your lost loved one. He knows about the plot they have on you. Nevertheless, the LORD Jesus Christ has already given you victory. Jesus Christ is your victory. No one can steal Him away from you. No one can take away the joy of the LORD Jesus from you (and yes, His joy is still inside of you even in your depression).

One of the things that keep me from retaliating the way my flesh wanted to in most cases was that in the midst of the betrayal I knew that God had already created me to be victorious. I knew deep in my heart that this kind of betrayal would have never taken place if God did not prepare a prepared place for me. My enemies who came in the form of some friends and family only confirmed God's plan for my life. If you really believed God's plan for your life, you would drop your pettiness and pick up your place, and place it back into the hands of the LORD Jesus Christ.

# The Temptation to Keep Your Distance

"Your body is here with me,
but your mind is on the other
side of town."- the O' Jays

There is an old saying, "If you feed a cat, they come back to your step. " Food is just a powerful as sex. On one episode of *Fresh Prince of Bel-Air*, Uncle Phil had a heart attack. His wife, Vivian, was in the waiting wrong filled with guilt and regret. She mentioned there were some nights when she was too tired to have sex, so she told him to go downstairs and fix himself something to eat. One sex addict reported, "Food is my number one favorite thing in the world." However, she had a weight problem. Therefore, to feel attracted during sex, she would binge eat.

As someone who loves to cook, and an African American at that, I know all about "Comfort food," from the smothered pork chops to the collard greens and smoked turkey. The kindest person will act out of character when they are hangry (defined as being bad-tempered or irritable as a result of hunger, according to the *Oxford Dictionary*). Co-workers will get together at the lunch table to discuss the gossip about each other or an employee, who they couldn't stand, who was recently fired.

Our food intake plays a big role in our mental health. Depression will increase or decrease our appetite. A person with a big appetite may not eat anything when they are nervous and anxious. Some clients of mine who struggle with cocaine addiction, for instance, will gain a lot of weight when they have been clean for a few months. New studies in neuro-counseling suggest a connection between our gut and brain. Dr. Vincent Pedre, MD, and author of *Happy Gut,* had some incredible insight on the "emotional gut":

"Your gut affects not only how your body feels, but it can also affect how you feel in your mind. it can be the source of immense suffering and, at the same time, the key to incredible wellness. Not only does treating the gut imbalances hold promise for resolving pain, inflammation, fatigue, allergic diseases, autoimmune diseases, and weight gain, but it also offers relief from brain-related disorders- from autism, attention deficit hyperactivity disorder, obsessive-compulsive disorder, and depression to dementia and even Parkinson's disease.

In fact, the gut is often referred to as the "second brain," and for good reason. Remarkable discoveries show how your gut can affect your mood and the way your brain functions. Even more surprising is how this is a two-way street; researchers have found that the brain also talks to the gut. .. Just as the brain has its own nervous system (the central nervous system, or CNS), the gut has the enteric nervous system (ENS).

Furthermore, food is also used as a manipulation tactic. Many were killed and set up in restaurants. Some wives and husbands have used food to poison their spouses. People who don't even like each other will agree to sit at a table together and go out to eat if they don't have to sit together. Yes, food makes the world go round.

Food is food to the full. However, food is a matter of life and death to those who are starving. All eleven of Joseph's brothers just knew that they wouldn't need him again, let alone see him again. However, when they thought that, their pantry was full, and the freezer was full of meat. It's easy to talk junk when food, shelter, and clothing are in abundance.

*"Now the famine was severe in the land. And when they had eaten the grain that they had brought from Egypt, their father said to them, "Go again, buy us a little food." But Judah said to him, "The man solemnly warned us, saying, 'You shall not see my face unless your brother is with you.' If you will send our brother with us, we will go down and buy you food. But if you will not send him, we will not go down, for the man said to us, 'You shall not see my face, unless your brother is with you.'" Israel said, "Why did you treat me so badly as to tell the man that you had another brother?" They replied, "The man questioned us carefully about ourselves and our kindred, saying, 'Is your father still alive? Do you have another brother?' What we told him was in answer to these questions. Could we in any way*

*know that he would say, 'Bring your brother down'?" And Judah said to Israel his father, "Send the boy with me, and we will arise and go, that we may live and not die, both we and you and also our little ones. I will be a pledge of his safety. From my hand you shall require him. If I do not bring him back to you and set him before you, then let me bear the blame forever. If we had not delayed, we would now have returned twice." Then their father Israel said to them, "If it must be so, then do this: take some of the choice fruits of the land in your bags, and carry a present down to the man, a little balm and a little honey, gum, myrrh, pistachio nuts, and almonds. Take double the money with you. Carry back with you the money that was returned in the mouth of your sacks. Perhaps it was an oversight. Take also your brother, and arise, go again to the man. May God Almightygrant you mercy before the man, and may he send back your other brother and Benjamin. And as for me, if I am bereaved of my children, I am bereaved." So the men took this present, and they took double the money with them, and Benjamin. They arose and went down to Egypt and stood before Joseph" (Genesis 43:1-15, ESV).*

# GUESS WHO'S COMING FOR DINNER?

The brothers of Joseph are in a place where they need Joseph again. They didn't know a day like this could happen. Often, the people who throw us away never think that Christ will position us in a place where they will need us again. Joseph is the only one they could think of who could help them; however, they didn't know this was Joseph. All they knew was that the governor told them not to come back to Egypt without his baby brother, Benjamin.

It is not a guarantee that they will eat. They have the money. They are even willing to take food with them on their trip to Egypt as a gift of hospitality. Yes, it's funny how life goes around. You never know where starvation will take you to. Jacob, on the other hand, is reluctant because he does not want to lose another son. Will they come back with food? Only God knows.

What if your past hurt showed up unannounced at your wedding? I'm not talking about your past objecting to you getting married. I'm talking about your past wanting your wife/ husband to have to carry the emotional baggage of your past hurt. What if you relocated to get away from the ex who hurt you only to have him follow you to another city emotionally? One expert said,

> "It's easy for a woman to get a man to leave
> her house; it's just hard to get him to leave
> her head."

Joseph was not starving, but his brothers were. Financially, he was doing fine with them. He even got married and started a family of his own. His brothers did not care to know if he was alive. They just wanted some plates to go even if the plate came from Joseph's house. Now is a good time to pause and tell you that **everyone who wants our food doesn't want us. They are just trying to stay alive by eating our food.**

> everyone who wants our food doesn't want us. They are just trying to stay alive by eating our food.

## LET'S EAT

*"When Joseph saw Benjamin with them, he said to the manager of his household, "These men will eat with me this noon. Take them inside the palace. Then go slaughter an animal, and prepare a big feast." So the man did as Joseph told him and took them into Joseph's palace.*

*The brothers were terrified when they saw that they were being taken into Joseph's house. "It's because of the money someone put in our sacks last time we were here," they said. "He plans to pretend that we stole it. Then he will seize us, make us slaves, and take our donkeys" (Genesis 43:16-18, NLT).*

### A Feast at Joseph's Palace

*"The brothers approached the manager of Joseph's household and spoke to him at the entrance to the palace. "Sir," they said, "we*

came to Egypt once before to buy food. But as we were returning home, we stopped for the night and opened our sacks. Then we discovered that each man's money—the exact amount paid—was in the top of his sack! Here it is; we have brought it back with us. We also have additional money to buy more food. We have no idea who put our money in our sacks." "Relax. Don't be afraid," the household manager told them. "Your God, the God of your father, must have put this treasure into your sacks. I know I received your payment." Then he released Simeon and brought him out to them. The manager then led the men into Joseph's palace. He gave them water to wash their feet and provided food for their donkeys. They were told they would be eating there, so they prepared their gifts for Joseph's arrival at noon. When Joseph came home, they gave him the gifts they had brought him, then bowed low to the ground before him. After greeting them, he asked, "How is your father, the old man you spoke about? Is he still alive?" "Yes," they replied. "Our father, your servant, is alive and well." And they bowed low again. Then Joseph looked at his brother Benjamin, the son of his own mother. "Is this your youngest brother, the one you told me about?" Joseph asked. "May God be gracious to you, my son." Then Joseph hurried from the room because he was *overcome with emotion for his brother. He went into his private room, where he broke down and wept. After washing his face, he came back out, keeping himself under control. Then he ordered, "Bring out the food!" The waiters served Joseph at his own table, and his brothers were served at a separate table. The Egyptians who ate with Joseph sat at their own table, because Egyptians despise Hebrews and refuse to eat with them. Joseph told each of his brothers where to sit, and to their amazement, he seated them according to age, from oldest to youngest. And Joseph filled their plates with food from his own table, giving Benjamin five times as much as he gave the others. So they feasted and drank freely with him"* (Genesis 43:19-34, NLT).

Have you ever watched the people who hurt you enjoy life as if you were not sitting there? Have you ever had someone hurt you and then tried to talk to you without apologizing? How do you enjoy the party with the perpetrator in the room? You haven't seen silent frustration until you're sitting in the same room with the people who hurt you, but act like they don't know you. Joseph was able to do it until he had to step out for a minute.

Psychologically speaking, we can conclude that Joseph deals with the pain by crying in isolation. Joseph is the kind of person that will feed his enemies but won't cry in front of them. Joseph is not shy; he is just not ready to reveal himself to them yet. However, he wants them to eat. Let me ask you a question, are you willing to feed your enemies?

## YOU CAN TOUCH MY FOOD, BUT YOU CAN'T TOUCH ME

When we are emotionally disconnected, we may not be aware of the signs and how they are manifested. Emotionally disconnected individuals can be very intriguing to the vulnerable because they give off mystery, appear to be calm and nonchalant, and are sometimes envied. I've seen mentally healthy individuals express jealousy for not being as quiet as the emotionally distant person. However, they are not aware that the calmness the emotionally unavailable individual gives off is the calm before the storm. According to Healthline Media, here are some signs you or someone you know is emotionally distant:

- Difficulty creating or maintaining personal relationships
- A lack of attention, or appearing preoccupied when around others
- Difficulty being loving or affectionate with a family member
- Avoiding people, activities, or places because they're associated with past trauma
- Reduced ability to express emotion
- Difficulty empathizing with another person's feelings
- Not easily sharing emotions or feelings
- Difficulty committing to another person or a relationship

- Not making another person a priority when they should be

Now there are quite a few factors that play into emotional disconnection. These factors entail past trauma, neglect, betrayal, abandonment, molestation, depression, shame, and low self-esteem. However, I want to talk about one that is very prevalent: "Don't Let them See You Sweat."

This slogan has a lot of pain, hurt, anger, and frustration attached to it. Truth be told no one has more emotions than someone who does not want to show them. Nevertheless, showing them is not a problem as much as it is embracing them. **Hiding our pain from the ones that we love or who love us may be common but it's not healthy. Joseph loved his brothers like he was never hurt by them, and oh how he cries while doing it.**

**Hiding our pain from the ones that we love or who love us may be common but it's not healthy. Joseph loved his brothers like he was never hurt by them, and oh how he cries while doing it.**

Now don't get this twisted, Joseph can still feed his brothers while he is trying not to let them see him sweat. Like Joseph, many of us substitute other things in place of showing vulnerability. Some fathers, for instance, may not know how to express their thoughts and feelings to their children but think paying bills and buying them gifts will take the place of that. Joseph is ready for them to eat at his table, but he is not ready to let them touch the sensitive parts of him.

## "I Say Go When I Mean Stay"

"Joseph ordered his house steward: "Fill the men's bags with food—all they can carry—and replace each one's money at the top of the bag. Then put my chalice, my silver chalice, in the top of the bag of the youngest, along with the money for his food." He did as Joseph ordered. At break of day the men were sent off with their donkeys. They were barely out of the city when Joseph said to his house steward, "Run after them. When you catch up with them, say, 'Why did you pay me back evil for good? This is the chalice my master drinks from; he also uses it for divination. This is outrageous!'" He caught up with them and repeated all this word for word. They said, "What is my master talking about? We would never do anything like that! Why, the money we found in our bags earlier, we brought back all the way from Canaan—do you think we'd turn right around and steal it back from your master? If that chalice is found on any of us, he'll die; and the rest of us will be your master's slaves."The steward said, "Very well then, but we won't go that far. Whoever is found with the chalice will be my slave; the rest of you can go free." They outdid each other in putting their bags on the ground and opening them up for inspection. The steward searched their bags, going from oldest to youngest. The chalice showed up in Benjamin's bag. They ripped their clothes in despair, loaded up their donkeys, and went back to the city. Joseph was still at home when Judah and his brothers got back. They threw themselves down on the ground in front of him. Joseph accused them: "How can you have done this? You have to know that a man in my position would have discovered this." Judah as spokesman for the brothers said, "What can we say, master? What *is* there to say? How can we prove our innocence?

God is behind this, exposing how bad we are. We stand guilty before you and ready to be your slaves—we're all in this together, the rest of us as guilty as the one with the chalice." "I'd never do that to you," said Joseph. "Only the one involved with the chalice will be my slave. The rest of you are free to go back to your father." Judah came forward. He said, "Please, master; can I say just one thing to you? Don't get angry. Don't think I'm presumptuous—you're the same as Pharaoh as far as I'm concerned. You, master, asked us, 'Do you have a father and a brother?' And we answered honestly, 'We have a father who is old and a younger brother who was born to him in his old age. His brother is dead and he is the only son left from that mother. And his father loves him more than anything.' "Then you told us, 'Bring him down here so I can see him.' We told you, master, that it was impossible: 'The boy can't leave his father; if he leaves, his father will die.' "And then you said, 'If your youngest brother doesn't come with you, you won't be allowed to see me.' "When we returned to our father, we told him everything you said to us. So when our father said, 'Go back and buy some more food,' we told him flatly, 'We can't. The only way we can go back is if our youngest brother is with us. We aren't allowed to even see the man if our youngest brother doesn't come with us.' "Your servant, my father, told us, 'You know very well that my wife gave me two sons. One turned up missing. I concluded that he'd been ripped to pieces. I've never seen him since. If you now go and take this one and something bad happens to him, you'll put my old gray, grieving head in the grave for sure.' "And now, can't you see that if I show up before your servant, my father, without the boy, this son with whom his life is so bound up, the moment he realizes the boy is gone, he'll die on the spot. He'll die of grief and we, your servants who are standing here before you, will have killed him. And that's not all. I got my father to release the boy to show him to you by promising, 'If I don't bring him back, I'll stand condemned before you, Father, all my life.' "So let me stay here as your slave, not this boy. Let the boy go back with his brothers. How can I go back to my father if the boy is not with me? Oh, don't make me go back and watch my father die in grief" (Genesis 44:1-34, MSG).

If you ask me, I'd say that Joseph is playing too many games. However, that is the conflict of someone who is trying to love those who despitefully used them. He loves them, but he is sending mixed messages at the same time. This is the temptation of being emotionally distant.

- "I want to be there, but I'm not ready to hear them tell me how they feel."
- "I want to forgive them, but I feel stupid for doing so."
- "I don't show it, but I love her very much."
- "I want to give my kids the love I never had, but I can't stop yelling."

I will never forget a neighbor of mine. He was physically abusive with one of his exes. By the time we arrived, she was gone. He begged his mother to call her and talk to her. Well, she came back over. She expressed to him that putting his hands on her was not acceptable. She was willing to take him back. Now ladies, before you get upset with a brother, I not telling any woman to stay with an abusive man. I mentioned this story because the same guy who wanted his mother to call her back over, so he could talk to her, was dead silent while she poured her heart out to him. That was the epitome of being emotionally distant.

Let's go to another extreme. I had an aunt who could not stand her husband's side of the family. She would even play sick when he wanted to see his family and brag about it. Well one day, his nephew was shot and killed. Later his body was discovered in the river. The whole family was distraught. However, instead of her having a heart for him in the face of death. She attended the funeral, but she came in time to hear the eulogist without telling my uncle she was coming.

## I Just Don't Want to Hurt No More

Emotionally distant individuals have more emotion than we think. They may not feel your pain because they are too busy feeling theirs. Yes. Emotionally disconnected individuals just don't want to hurt anymore. Joseph is not evil. He is a man of integrity with a bleeding heart. He just met evil too early at the hands of his brothers. Nevertheless, the evil that he met could not get rid of the love that was in his heart. He doesn't know how to deal with his emotions in a healthy way. He does what he knows best. He cries in the dark.

Judah is pleading for the mercy of Joseph (Genesis 44) not realizing it's Joseph. Joseph does not want to harm his brother or brothers, but the only way that he knows how to deal with his emotions. Joseph has his brothers in the dark because he is in the dark with his emotions. Who knows. Maybe Joseph wanted his brothers to feel the anxiety of not knowing what would happen to the next moment of their lives as they left him in the pit wondering what would happen to his life. Joseph is right in the room with his brothers, but he is hiding the pain. At least he is making the effort.

## How Long Can You Stay Away?

I want to talk to those of you, who the LORD Jesus Christ has led to reading this chapter, and who have left those you love because you were not emotionally available. I want to outline three scenarios of cases why we leave people in the dark because of the pain that we feel in our own hearts:

- **Competing with Who You Should Be Bonding With**- I never will forget watching an episode of Iyanla Vanzant, where a mother was raped by her uncle. As a result of that trauma, she started seeing women. One of the women she was sleeping with was her daughter's woman as well. When this secret came out in the open, her daughter stated that she always felt she competed with her mother. However, despite how many tears ran down her daughter's face, the mother remained stoic and cold. Now, there was a moment where the stoic mother exploded to tell her daughter how disrespectful she was, not realizing her daughter was the spitting image of her.

Are you competing with who you should be bonding with? There are talk shows where fathers are sleeping with their son's wives, and mothers are sleeping with their daughter's boyfriends. What is wrong with these families? They are looking for the wrong outlet to heal emotional wounds. There are families where siblings are competing with their parent's "favorite child." There are friends who have turned their friendship into a competition over lust for power. Don't lose what you have trying to get something that you don't need.

- **Running Away from Responsibilities due to being Overwhelmed & Feeling Insecure-** This is normally prevalent in homes with absent fathers. All men who walk out are not walking out because they don't want to see their children. Some fathers walked out because they never saw a father in action. Some have walked out due to anger, thinking "if I never had a dad my kids won't either." Still, other fathers have walked out due to feeling insecure about their capability to be a dad.

Now, your issue may not be with fatherhood, but what area of your life are you emotionally distant from because facing the responsibilities is overwhelming? Are you running away from the consequences of your actions because you're too embarrassed about being found out? I want you to know that Jesus is a God of justice, but he is also a God of mercy. Just because the LORD Jesus Christ wanted you to turn yourself in does not mean He is against you. It means He is for justice while He extends mercy at the same time. If you can trust Christ's judgment, you can also have faith in His mercy.

- **Playing Games in Relationships-** This one is very common. It's everywhere. This is settling for control over love. This is settling for sex over intimacy. This is settling for lust over loyalty. When we have given up on love, we become skilled at breaking the hearts of those who fall in love with us. I once heard a woman say, "I can make a man think he is in love with me." That's too many games. That woman has been heartbroken since then and has recently been divorced. **I don't care how good you think you are at playing games with someone's heart, there is someone who can play the game better than you.**

Please know that there is no peace in playing games with the hearts of others. Why? For one, it will make us suspicious of someone we love playing games with us when we finally decide to settle down. Hear me real good, stop while you're ahead. If you only knew how much of a re- ward the LORD Jesus Christ is in our lives, you would stop playing games.

## ALL ABOUT THE BENJAMIN

Have you noticed that Joseph seems to be concerned about showing special favor to only one brother although he loves all of them? For starters, Benjamin was the youngest son next to Joseph. Secondly, Benjamin was his full-blood brother (their mother was Rachel who died giving birth to Benjamin). We will never know why Joseph gives him special treatment. The Bible never tells us. However, one thing we know for certain is Benjamin was not like his other brothers. He was just caught in the middle. Joseph might have felt that Benjamin did not want to be a part of that and didn't know how to help. Only God knows.

Nevertheless, Benjamin makes it hard for Joseph to be emotionally distant because Joseph misses him. I want to pause right now and talk to all of us who have a Benjamin in our life. Benjamin may be a child that is innocent but gets the short end of his angry mother's temper for looking like the father she is still mad at. Benjamin may be the one the friend you envy because her skin is lighter than yours although that friend would give you the shirt off her back. Benjamin represents the child you paid to send away because you did not want the embarrassment of having a child out of wedlock. While you have a chance to mend these broken relationships, please get it right today.

## A Lesson on Missing Who You Don't Need

Listen, feelings are deceitful. Feelings should be acknowledged but that doesn't mean they are right. Feelings of loneliness will tempt you to call exes who you should let remain asleep. Feelings of guilt will make you think you were wrong to leave the narcissist who beat you all over the house. **Just because you miss them doesn't mean you should want them.** Oftentimes, we think missing someone equates to being in love with them. Truth be told, sometimes it's not that you love them. You just miss the way that they loved (or lusted) you.

Now is a good time to ask you if you have learned to be alone. Learning to be alone requires being able to trust the presence of God in the face of the absence of your favorite person. Being alone requires challenging those insecurities that make you think that you are useless without the one you miss. They do not complete you. You are complete in Christ, according to Colossians 2:10. You have made their life your life and their goals your goal. What do you want to do? What has Christ purposed in your heart to do that is pleasing unto him? Do that. Never forget, what the older generation told us, "Only what you do for Christ will last."

## "I WAS JUST TESTING YOU"

Do you know how many of us are turning people into emotionally distant individuals by testing their loyalty? You don't call them just to see if they will call you. Waiting twenty-four minutes before you respond to their text message. Pretending that you were sick just to see if they would cancel their plans. The list goes on and on. Consequently, sooner or later you'll end up disappointed, and they'll end up getting tired of not knowing there was a pop quiz today. Joseph tested his brothers' loyalty by playing money on their backs. Hear me: **You'll never get loyalty from a thief by hiding money in their pockets.**

> **You'll never get loyalty from a thief by hiding money in their pockets.**

If you have to do all that to see how loyal they are, you're doing too much. You have to seek therapy for your trust issues; know who you cannot trust again; have reasonable expectations for the people you allow in your circle.

# BEING EMOTIONALLY DISTANT FROM CHRIST

I will never forget having a client battling substance use disorder. He was open and honest about his drug problem, but he wanted to spend an ample amount of time talking about God. He discussed with me how angry he was with Jesus Christ for not protecting him from sexual molestation and the death of his friend. He was at a point where he still believed there is a God. However, he didn't believe that God was involved in the pain and hurt of people. He felt God only remained on the throne.

I explained to him as I will to you that the Bible is clear that Jesus Christ, the LORD God, can be touched. Christ wanted us to know that He cares about the affairs of men when God came to earth, manifesting Himself in the flesh, in the person of Jesus Christ (1 Timothy 3:16). Hebrews 4:15 teaches us clearly that Jesus Christ can feel our pain:

> *"Now that we know what we have- Jesus, this great High Priest with ready access to God- lets not let it slip through our fingers. We don't have a priest who is out of touch with our reality. He's been through weakness and testing, experienced it all- all but the sin. So let's walk right up to him and get what he is so ready to give. Take the mercy, accept the help"* *(Hebrews 4:14-16, MSG).*

Like my client, you might be saying, "Jesus was not sexually molested. How can He know how I feel?" You're right. However, Jesus Christ can feel the pain the sexually molested how felt. Christ is not so much God that he cannot feel. The devil may be tempting you to be emotionally distant from Christ because satan wants you to believe that God does not care. That devil lied to you again! While you are reading this with tears coming down your eyes, the LORD Jesus Christ can hear your cries. I will leave you with this scripture that I left with my client:

> *"O Lord, you have examined my heart and know everything about me. You know when I sit down or stand up. You know my thoughts even when I'm far away. You see me when I travel and when I rest at home. You know everything I do. You know what I am going to say even before I say it, Lord. You go before me and follow me. You place your hand of blessing on my head. Such knowledge is too wonderful for me, too great for me to understand!*
>
> *I can never escape from your Spirit! I can never get away from your presence! If I go up to heaven, you are there; if I go down to the grave, you are there. If I ride the wings of the morning, if I dwell by the farthest oceans, even there your hand will guide me, and your strength will support me. I could ask the darkness to hide me and the light around me to become night— but even in darkness I cannot hide from you. To you the night shines as bright as day. Darkness and light are the same to you.*
>
> *You made all the delicate, inner parts of my body and knit me together in my*

mother's womb. Thank you for making me so wonderfully complex! Your workmanship is marvelous—how well I know it. You watched me as I was being formed in utter seclusion, as I was woven together in the dark of the womb. You saw me before I was born. Every day of my life was recorded in your book. Every moment was laid out before a single day had passed.

How precious are your thoughts about me, O God. They cannot be numbered! I can't even count them; they outnumber the grains of sand! And when I wake up, you are still with me!

O God, if only you would destroy the wicked! Get out of my life, you murderers! They blaspheme you; your enemies misuse your name. O Lord, shouldn't I hate those who hate you? Shouldn't I despise those who oppose you? Yes, I hate them with total hatred, for your enemies are my enemies.

Search me, O God, and know my heart; test me and know my anxious thoughts. Point out anything in me that offends you, and lead me along the path of everlasting life" (Psalms 139, NLT).

## WHAT DOES THE TEMPTATION TO KEEP MY DISTANCE HAVE TO DO WITH MY DESTINY?

Many of you reading this love on a level that you don't always get back. It's not because no one wants to love you, but you keep expecting it from people who don't have the capacity to love on that level. I know you want from a mother that cannot give. Maybe you want closure from an ex that refuses to give it. Or, you want an apology from the ones who you already have proven your innocence and have the evidence of your innocence right in their hand.

Hear me real good. The more you look for the wrong hearts to heal your heart, you will continue to push the right people out of your heart. Trust Christ and the people He has al- ready and will send into your life. In the meantime, forgive those who hurt you. Take time to heal before you allow insecurities to push you into the wrong bed from someone from social media you met an hour ago. Delete those numbers that are your cushion on a lonely night from your phone.

Keep in mind, you can be in a place of blessing and not enjoy it because you've allowed the LORD Jesus Christ to bless your finance without letting him in to heal your heart. You have to settle for looking good because you don't believe that God can make you feel good. You have so much baggage that you settled for bags of crack cocaine, fentanyl, and heroin to numb the pain. Or maybe you have bottled up so much pain that you've turned to the bottle. If you cannot trust Christ with your emotions, you really don't trust Him at all. Jesus is not just the God of the Church; Jesus is the God of your emotions.

You are not a victim although you might have been victimized. You are victorious in Christ even when you don't feel victorious. Don't you ever forget that! Now let's go to the next chapter. Before you do, give the LORD Jesus Christ praise for being victorious in Him.

# The Temptation to Keep Our Secrets to Ourselves

"Every man has his secret sorrows
which the world knows not, and
oftentimes we call a man cold when
he is only sad." -Henry Wadsworth

They think you talk too much. They watch what they say when you're in the room. They even have nicknames for you because they think you're the loose lips that sank ships. I wish I had a chance to speak to them and let them know that even the most talkative person has some secrets that they have not shared. Yes, we tell people what we want them to know, and some- times the secrets we share, with the people we choose to share them with, are sometimes shared to manipulate with guilt. Nevertheless, secrets hide in the heart.

Contrary to popular belief, all secrets are not bad. Nevertheless, good secrets can be damaging if held for too long. Haven't you noticed television shows that get high ratings are shows with secrets? Haven't you noticed that talk shows that have the best secrets stay on the air longer? Songs, where one rapper exposes another rapper, will reach the top of the Billboard charts. Yes, secrets are juicy to the outsiders who get the gossip. However, secrets are detrimental to th person who continues to hold them in.

Joseph has now seen God show him favor beyond comparison. He is no longer the seventeen-year-old boy who was misunderstood by his family, hated by his brothers, placed in a pit, and ultimately sold into slavery. Oh no. The brother can say that dreams really do come true, especially when they come from God. He is not the prince of Egypt. Which woman wouldn't want him? Which guy wouldn't want to be one of his homeboys? Even his brothers ended up coming to him for food. Nevertheless, Joseph had secrets.

## There is Something You Aren't Telling Me

*"Blessed is the one whose transgression is forgiven, whose sin is covered. Blessed is the man against whom the LORD counts no iniquity, and in whose spirit there is no deceit. For when I kept silent, my bones wasted away through my groaning all day long. For day and night your hand was heavy upon me; my strength was dried up as by the heat of summer. Selah. I acknowledged my sin to you, and I did not cover my iniquity; I said, "I will confess my transgressions to the LORD," and you forgave the iniquity of my sin. Selah"* (Psalms 32:1-5, ESV).

The above passage is King David telling us about the blessed life of someone who tells God about their secret sins. David was a man after God's own heart with secret sins. David in Hebrew means "beloved of God," yet he kept secrets from God. Now the question is how can it be a secret if God is all-knowing? The LORD Jesus Christ is all-knowing because He is the almighty. However, he wants us to come to him. **We haven't seen a real talk with Jesus until we can tell Him about the sins that we are hiding from him.**

> **We haven't seen a real talk with Jesus until we can tell Him about the sins that we are hiding from him.**

Keep in mind, David was a believer. He was not a sinner writing this. He was a man of God writing this. He talks about how keeping his sins a secret made him ill until he made up his mind to confess his transgressions to the LORD. When I was growing up in Church we used to sing "I must tell Jesus. Tell Him all about my troubles." **Yes, we were good at telling Jesus about our troubles but we didn't tell Him about our secrets.** Let me ask you a question. When was the last time you had God answer a prayer regarding your secrets?

> **Yes, we were good at telling Jesus about our troubles but we didn't tell Him about our secrets.**

Many of us are suffering in plain sight with people all around us because we are too embarrassed to ask for help. Maybe we came from a family of judgmental relatives that we don't want to go to. Or you're so used to keeping the light off of yourself by talking about others that you have become comfortable with distracting yourself from your secrets. Or, you may have heard how your friends put others down that you have thought twice about sharing your secrets with them.

## Where is the Safest Place to Take My Secrets?

Joseph went to the top, and he went with God on his side. However, he took his secrets with him. Contrary to popular belief, it is possible to go to the next level and still have secrets. It's possible to go from employee to entrepreneur and have secrets. It's common to go from stripper to wife and have secrets. It's not an oddity to go from local preacher to international itinerary Bishop and have secrets. Secrets have purchased their passports with us to travel with us all around the world.

How do our secrets travel so well with us without making the metal detector go off before we get on the next flight to our destiny? They rely on our "self-talk." We distract ourselves with what we tell ourselves about our secrets. We say things to ourselves like:

- "What they don't know won't hurt them."
- "I'm not going to feel bad for cheating on him because he cheated on me."
- "I'm did what was best for them."
- "I will cross that bridge when I get to it."

Joseph's secrets, however, are not secrets of sins. They are secrets of betrayal by his flesh and blood. He is not in the palace gossiping about them. He is running Egypt like he has never been hurt. He is helping others with their dreams while he is crying in silence over his secrets.

We have noticed that even after reuniting with his brothers, he wasn't ready to talk about it. He has never learned coping skills from a therapist, nor has he learned assertive training skills from a psychologist. A psychiatrist has not prescribed him antidepressants. Joseph only hiding place, up until Genesis chapter 45, has been God.

## It's Still A Secret If You Haven't Told it to the Right One

Now let's backtrack. The Bible does give us one suspect that Joseph vented to. Remember the butler, back in Genesis chapter 40, to who Joseph revealed his secrets to? Let's review what Joseph said when he spilled his secret to the butler:

> *"Only remember me when things are going well with you again- tell Pharaoh about me and get me out of this place. I was kidnapped from the land of the Hebrews. And since I've been here, I've done nothing to deserve being put in this hole" (Genesis 40 13-15, MSG).*

Now let's dissect a few things from the above passage. Notice Joseph does not tell the full story. He does mention he was stolen but does not mention who kidnapped him. He keeps his brothers anonymous. Can

**Have you been protecting the name of the person or people who hurt you?**

I ask you another question? **Have you been protecting the name of the person or people who hurt you?** Now, this can go both ways. The negative side of this question is gossiping about them, spreading lies, and defamation of character out of hurt, anger, and frustration that fueled our flesh to get back at them.

The only problem with this is that it shows who your faith is in. The LORD Jesus Christ has you reading this book for a reason. When you can develop the "Christ-Confidence" to treat the people who hurt you right, God will give us peace that surpasses all understanding. The Bible clearly encouraged us not to *"Fret not yourself because of evildoers; be not envious of wrong-doers! For they will soon fade like the grass and wither like the green herb. Trust in the LORD, and do good; dwell in the land and befriend faithfulness"* (Psalms 37:1-3, ESV).

The other side of protecting the name of the person who hurt us is that we are secretly carrying pain and trauma inside of us that is perpetuating itself. Growing up in the African American community, many of us were taught that "what goes on in this house stays in this house." However, you must get help for the trauma you have been through. That molestation you never talked about; the rape you suppressed has your husband questioning himself when he constantly gets turned down for sex because you get flashbacks and nightmares (which are symptoms of post-traumatic stress disorder or PTSD) every time he touches you.

I want to encourage you to know that there is nothing wrong with seeking therapy. How long are you going to continue to suffer in silence regarding the secrets that are hurting you because you want to protect someone's name? I'm not telling you to go live on Facebook. I'm telling you to open up to a therapist. Additionally, as a licensed counselor, whose expertise is in self-esteem, I would add that it's vital that you seek out a therapist who understands the role of self-esteem or the lack thereof in relation to PTSD and trauma (for more information on how low self-esteem affects everyday life- check out my book *Christ Confident: Finally Placing Our Confidence in the Right ONE*).

When we heal, we can inspire others who are suffering in silence. Trauma grows in silence. Depression destroys when no one is around. Suicidal ideation takes us out in isolation. Turn your trauma and PTSD into a testimony that the LORD Jesus Christ can heal, deliver and set free even now. The molester or rapist has used pseudo-guilt (that means guilt that comes from manipulation or lack of understanding) to keep you quiet. Or some perpetrators will afford you with hush money, but I want you to know there is no wealth like the benefits of getting the secrets out.

## LEAKED VIDEOS

One thing about those cameras, they do not lie. Screenshots, hidden cameras, and even phone trackers make investigations less strenuous but the life of the unjust person harder. Technology has afforded us great opportunities but it also exposed things we wish to have never seen. Additionally, it has been said that the human eye is like a camera. When my grandmother meant business, should say, "Let me look into your eyes." It has also been said that the eye is the seat of the soul.

You can't look at his success and tell that Joseph has been through trauma. One cannot look at his palace and see that he has spent time in the pit. Nor can one look at his bank account and see what it cost him to tell his dreams. Nevertheless, when we look into the eyes of Joseph, his brother Judah pleads for peace, Joseph could not stand it any longer. He begins to cry. Tears started to fall. Secrets started to come out. "Joseph could no longer keep his composure in front of all his attendants,[a] so he called out, 'Send everyone away from me!' No one was with him when he revealed his identity to his brothers. But he wept so loudly that the Egyptians heard it, and also Pharaoh's household heard it" (Genesis 45:1-2, CSB).

## BEING STRONG ALL THE TIME HURTS

I never will forget a friend of mine, who I would say had a rough life. She had been verbally abused by her father, and every boyfriend she had cheated on her to the degree to which she started cheating back. Consequently, her self-esteem took a hit. Nevertheless, on the outside, she looked like she had it all together. She was considered the tough one in the fight. She didn't take any junk from anyone. However, once she called she would be crying, saying, "I really get tired of being strong."

I could understand where Joseph is coming from. He was vulnerable with his brothers at seventeen when he shared his dreams, and it nearly cost him his life. You can be just as hurt from opening up about your dreams as you are opening up about your secrets. Dreams will reveal who is really happy for you. Telling your dreams will identify whose words are genuine but the body language wasn't lying. Joseph learned to be quiet about his dream; nevertheless, little did his brothers know- they are now living in it.

Being strong on the outside has its advantages. It keeps people out of our business. It makes us look like nothing is wrong. People admire your strength (not knowing what is really going on inside). However, secrets cause depression, anxiety, nightmares, low self-esteem, and even ideations of suicide. God used the pleas of his brother Judah to get Joseph to finally admit that he is still alive to tell the story of his past. Joseph began to cry.

## THE FATHER THAT HEARS IN SECRET

**Believe me when I say, our relationship with the LORD Jesus Christ deepens when we can bring our secrets to him.** For every secret that you are carrying, God has a secret place for you to find in Him. "He that dwells in the secret place of the most high shall abide under the shadow of the Almighty" (Psalms 91:1). You have been so protective of your secrets that it is not safe for the people in your life who love you.

Jesus Christ knows what goes through your mind when your secrets come up. He knows why you have been working so hard to keep that secret to yourself. However, you must tell the truth. Secrets are lies when the child who has a right to know who his father is has it hidden from him. Secrets are lies when you allow your daughter to go around the uncle that molested you when you were a child. Secrets are lies when your husband doesn't know you kissed his homie. Secrets are lies when you have a family and a secret account your spouse knows nothing about.

I dare you to trust Christ with your secrets. You don't have to reveal them alone. When you tell the truth, the truth, who is the LORD Jesus Christ himself will show up and stand beside you. Now I want to give you a caveat when you finally come clean about the secrets you have been carrying, it most likely will get ugly. You may be met with angry outbursts, abandonment, called a liar, blocked off social media, taken out of the wedding, and even exposed on social media. Nevertheless, if God is for you, who can be against you?

## What Does the Temptation to Keep My Secrets to Myself Have to Do with My Destiny?

The word of God teaches us that God is a Spirit (John 4:24), and those of us who want to worship Him must worship Him in spirit and truth. How can we be spirit filled and die with untold secrets inside of us? Unfortunately, many of us do it daily. I know you may be carrying guilt, shame, fear, and remorse due to the secrets you have carried for so long. You may be thinking that by now, you have a lot to lose. Please whatever you do, don't let that secret eat you away another day.

Secrets are the things that we don't tell ourselves. Read that twice. Read it again. Read it one more time. We lie to ourselves every day to be at peace of mind about the secrets we suppress. You may be saying no one will find out. This is 2022, you'll be amazed at what can come out. It's better to tell the truth out of your own mouth before someone else tells it for you. What if your secrets get exposed when you're at the height of your God-ordained destiny? What if your child has to find out your secrets at forty that you should have told them at fourteen? You and I no longer have the right to remain silent. The secrets we won't tell are the secrets that satan will use against us. Don't give the devil any more rope to hang you. The LORD Jesus Christ has already hung on the cross for every secret you are carrying.

# The Temptation to Neglect Your Responsibility

"We don't have to answer to Christ
for how people treat us; we have to
answer to Christ for how we treat
them." -Anonymous Christian

I once heard someone that "Everyone is a Christian until it gets biblical." Truth be told there are scriptures, commands, and passages in the Bible that Christ expects us to obey in our daily walk with him. However, that fleshly mind of ours wants to do what it wants to do. One of the things that Christ has asked us to do was love our enemies (Matthew 5:44). What do you do, however, when that enemy is in your bloodline? One of the fights about loving your enemies is to believe in the family to help you fight some enemies.

There was a time when our grandparents were the glue that held the family together, especially in the African-American culture. Nevertheless, when some of our grandparents passed away, the family was never the same again. Joseph has been lied to by Potiphar's wife and never mentions it again in scripture. However, getting over what his brothers did was hard. He has a hard time being in the same room long enough without getting emotional. Nevertheless, God still wants Joseph to act like a believer after everything they have done to him.

## FIGHTING THE GOOD FIGHT OF FAITH IS NOT A FAIR FIGHT

You haven't seen faith in action until it's time to forgive. You have to trust the LORD Jesus Christ to forgive people. God never said what the brothers did to Joseph was right. In fact, when we study the life of Joseph, there is nowhere in his story where God speaks. We see God's love through Joseph's response of love and care after being left and abandoned by his family. Can I tell you one reason why I can love my enemies is that I have learned that as much as I thought they were using me- I realized all my life God was using them.

I am sure that there was no way that Joseph could forgive his brothers without faith in God. In fact, Joseph's faith in God was his sanity through it all. However, that did not change the fact that it doesn't feel like loving our enemies is fair after everything they did to us. How can you be my family and enemy at the same time? How can you be my wife and out to get me for my insurance policy at the same time? How can you be my child

> **When you do your best to live by the word of God, and people still do you wrong- know that it's more than just personal. It's a spiritual battle.**

and forge my signature to satisfy your selfish greed at the same time? When it comes to the life of Joseph, this was more than just personal; it was spiritual. **When you do your best to live by the word of God, and people still do you wrong- know that it's more than just personal. It's a spiritual battle.**

What is interesting is that God never gave Joseph a dream explaining why he went through all of this. He does, however, give him a dream about his brothers bowing down to him. Nevertheless, he did not know they would bow down to him when they were in need. This was more than the need that brought them together; it was the purpose of God that brought them all together. Joseph's dreams being fulfilled was more about Joseph being blessed; it was about blessing his brothers with what God blessed him with.

## Your Obligation is Your Blessing

Joseph's heart was not designed to turn his brothers down. He loved them. When you love those who have wronged you, your heart and mind are always at war. Heart says, "be there for them." Your mind says, "They left you hanging. Forget them." Your heart says, "Go visit them in the hospital." Your mind says, "They can rot in that hospital for all I care." Oh yes, the flesh doesn't want to do that. Check this out: Joseph's destiny was not the palace. Joseph's destiny was to feed his brothers.

A destiny that doesn't entail loving your enemies is not of God. A destiny that neglects the responsibility to the poor is a waste of the resources that Christ has given us. A destiny that can only love those who left us is not Christlike. A destiny that doesn't realize that Jesus Christ was in control of the people who hurt me will germinate bitterness and resentment. From the moment Joseph reconnected with his brother; he has been preoccupied with making sure that they all eat- even his father.

## You Go Your Way, and I'll Go Mine

Many people have gotten away from toxic people but are left with the mentality of the perpetrators' toxicity. They finally left your life, but they are still in your head. They are no longer physically abusing you, but your self-esteem is filled with their emotional and verbal abuse that continues to affect how you receive love now. Are you living the rest of your life out of the emotional and verbal wounds of your past?

Sabotage is at its best when we ruin our present by acting like where we came from. Are you battling with relinquishing control to your husband because all your exes in the past were domineering and controlling? Are you distrustful of the wife Christ gave you because exes in the past you gave all your money to used you? **It's a special kind of torment to be mentally tortured by a voice in the past that you are no longer geographically with.**

> It's a special kind of torment to be mentally tortured by a voice in the past that you are no longer geographically with.

Furthermore, some of us have completed the internal healing, gotten our Christ-Confidence back, and finally left the toxic people in our past where they belong. The only problem is that the past can almost smell when you move on. Joseph has moved on. He did not go his way; he was sent into slavery. Nevertheless, he made it to the palace. Unfortunately, his brothers followed him to the palace. You haven't been stalked until someone who told you they were through with you needs you.

There are family members who cursed you out but still watch your Facebook page through a fake account. Some people will never support you but are constantly looking up information on you. They will never come to your event, but trust and believe they are calling the next day, asking their spies who went what happen. Nevertheless, some of them aren't coming around you because of how they talked about you. Nevertheless, there are some who have treated you like Alabama trash and dared to come around you, text you, or send someone to let you know they are in trouble because they are in a place of need where they aren't too proud to beg.

## Tell Them I'm Not Home

They say you cannot stop the bill collector from calling, you just don't have to answer the phone. That is a financial game that I would not play if I were you. We all have one or a few individuals that we have learned to live without. However, what do you do when they knock on your door, not to say sorry, but to ask for another favor? I know you're not trying to hear, "What would Jesus do," or "Be the bigger person." I hear you, but let me ask you a question. Did you think that you would be betrayed on the level that you were betrayed on and not be needed by the people who betrayed you? Did you think that they were going to try to destroy your character and God not position you to be in a place to have exactly what they need?

Notice, the devil is never mentioned anywhere in the story of Joseph. God was the CEO of Joseph's life. Everything his deceitful brothers did to Joseph was setting Joseph up to be in a place where he could feed them. Have you ever wondered why people betray you and sleep like a baby, but you just get convicted by the holy spirit for entertaining the thought of retaliation? I want you to know that the bigger the betrayal, the bigger the blessing. Christ is not taking the people who hurt you where he is taking you. God wants you to know that you still have a responsibility to be there for the person who hurt you because you have to let your light shine even when others have left you in the dark.

## WHEN THEY DON'T MAKE IT EASY TO LOVE THEM

Have you ever tried to help an ungrateful enemy? Have you ever tried to be there for some- one who you know in your heart would not be there for you? Sometimes, it is hard in our human mind to do this when we know they are stubborn and set in their ways. Sometimes they take our kindness for weakness. They think that we don't or won't get tired because we loved on a level their insecurity and ego are too blind to see. How do you deal with people who are back in your life, but refused to change?

Joseph has let his brothers back into his life while they don't realize it was him. I am sure that if they were not in need- they would have left Joseph alone, once they realized it was him. What I find intriguing is that we read nowhere in the life of Joseph where his brothers apologized. **Yes, you have**

**Yes, you have a responsibility to heal even though they have neglected their obligation to apologize.**

**a responsibility to heal even though they have neglected their obligation to apologize.**

Truth be told, there is no way we can truly be accountable to Christ if we neglect our enemies, especially if they are someone we once considered family or friends. Some people are not going to make it easy for us to love them. This is why **we truly cannot love our enemies without the confidence that comes from the Holy Ghost.** The LORD Jesus Christ made it clear to us that we get no brownie points from him if we only love those who love us (Luke 6:32). That's why we have the comfort of the Holy Ghost to assist us in loving those who are difficult to love.

There are some men, for example, that are trying to be good fathers to their child/children, but the mother is hurt and using the child/children as a way to punish the father. I want to say to any mother reading this book knows that you have a right to be hurt, but you have a responsibility to make sure your child/children have a father in their life. Now there are cases where the father might have molested the child or physically abused you. Nevertheless, what about the man who is a good father although he may not be the best husband? Kids should not have to suffer over issues that their parents should rectify for the sake of the children.

Or you may be bitter that you never had a father in your own life. Why pass down that mentality to another generation? Why not have

> we truly cannot love our enemies without the confidence that comes from the Holy Ghost.

> The Holy Ghost healed me to be able to be to my future children what my father was not to me.

faith in the LORD Jesus Christ and break the cycle? I refuse not to be a father because mine was not around. **The Holy Ghost healed me to be able to be to my future children what my father was not to me.** If you're healed, why be bitter then?

## MAN SHALL NOT LIVE BY BREAD ALONE

Joseph's brothers were hungry and needed a seat at Joseph's table. If Joseph would have said no, his brothers, along with his father, were going to die due to starvation by the famine. Now they are in a place where the only person they could depend on is the one they did wrong. The only one that could help them was the one they did not believe in. Be careful who you mistreat because we will all need to eat sooner or later.

Now the question arises, what will Joseph eat while they eat? While his brothers wanted to live off the food that Joseph was going to supply, Joseph was living off the word of God. The question is how is Joseph living off a word from God from the Bible that wasn't written yet? The answer is simple: Joseph's dream was a word from God. Let me pause and ask you are your dreams a God dream? Do you want the business because you want to be successful according to the will of God for your life or you want to prove a point to someone in your past who told you that you would never amount to anything? **Any dream you go after that did not come from God will ultimately become the nightmare of your life.**

As I studied the life of Joseph, I could not help but look at my own life. I know for a fact that the only thing that kept me from really retaliating against my enemies is knowing that God spoke a word over my life and none of them had the power to change it. I still believed that I would see the goodness of the LORD Jesus in the land of the living when it was all said and done. That is why I didn't mind looking bad for a few minutes because I knew that God would make me look good for a lifetime.

Jesus said to Satan one day, "Man shall not live by bread alone but by every word that proceedeth out of the mouth of God" (Matthew 4:4). Jesus ad that statement when the enemy was trying to tempt him to forget who he was (Jesus is the bread of life). You cannot get through depression, anxiety, and fear without a good diet of the word of God! The word of God knows us more and even better than we know ourselves.

> ## WHAT DOES THE TEMPTATION TO NEGLECT MY RESPONSIBILITIES HAVE TO DO WITH MY DESTINY?
>
> What good is it to come to the end of your destiny, and all you were able to say is that you had fun, but neglected the people that the LORD Jesus Christ placed in your pathway?
>
> We have a responsibility to utilize every gift that the LORD Jesus Christ has placed on the inside of us. Moreover, our enemies are able to say they have experienced those gifts.

Your destiny is all about the responsibility you have to reach who Jesus wants you to reach even if it means reaching those who plotted against you.

# The Temptation to Wish You Were Somebody Else

"I am what God says I am. I am more
than a Conqueror through Him that
loves me." -Dorothy Norwood

How can a man with a good woman ruin it in fifteen minutes with a couple of screenshots? How can a woman complains about not having a good man while talking to a good man only to friend-zone him later? How can a woman who is envied and hated by other women at the same time feel ugly and develop an eating disorder? What makes a person of good character lose it all to drug addiction? How can the soul-stirring preacher end up in the swingers club on Sunday night?

The above questions are what the Apostle James can give us an answer for. He calls it "double-minded." He writes to the early church, "A double-minded man is unstable in all his ways" (James 1:8, KJV). That means **when a person is not in harmony with who the LORD Jesus Christ called us to be,**

**every detour we take will lead to a dead end.** Furthermore, one cannot be unstable in all his/her ways without thoughts and feelings of believing they are less than who Christ has called them to be.

This is spiritual warfare at its finest. For satan to bring us down through the conduits of temptation he has to make us think we are inferior and less than others. Yes, self-doubt is the mother of misery and the slippery slope to being defeated by temptation. Think for a moment. You are not calling that married man to see how his wife is doing. It's even bigger than sex. You already have sex toys on your nightstand. You're calling a married man because you don't believe that God will send you your man.

That woman you are thinking about marrying treats you like garbage. She talks down to you. She even allows her kids to disrespect you. Nevertheless, deep down inside you know you're only staying because you did not think you could get her in the first place. **When we have no Christ-confidence, we can get anything that Satan has to offer.**

## Your Confidence Fight is a Faith Fight

Listen to me and listen to me good. Every temptation in your life is after one thing: your faith in your Christ-predestined identity. The devil cannot change who God says that we are.

However, if he can get us to second-guess ourselves for just two good minutes, we will be calling ex-lovers we thought we were finished with, going back to old jobs that we took money under the table for, swinging by old neighborhoods that got us arrested, and taking detours on the road to our divine destiny.

Trust me when I tell you child of God the fight not to backslide is really about your insecurities in areas you don't believe God in. This area is very familiar to you too. The devil knows that he cannot shake your faith in those other areas you never doubted yourself in. However, you're not over the words of the playground bullies that have you weighing yourself on the scale many years later. The devil sat back and watches you get married, but he waits till you feel lonely and then reminds you of the escorts in your neighborhood.

It's not that you don't want to be free or want to be delivered. The real issue you don't think Jesus is God enough to build your confidence in Him in areas of weakness in your life that existed for so long. You relapsed and went back to the bottle because you have given up on the saving power of God and even left rehab against medical advice. You're tempted to abort the baby because you don't think you could be a good mother.

**TO LOSE CONFIDENCE IN YOURSELF IS TO LOSE TRUST IN THE GOD IN YOU THAT PROMISED TO NEVER LEAVE YOU.**

*"Greater is he that is in you than he that is in the world"* (1 John 4:4, KJV). Many of us who wrestle with the anxiety of self-doubt are questioning God's presence and love in our lives.

Even the twelve disciples of Jesus Christ even asked the LORD Jesus did he care if they die:

> "And the same day, when the even was come, he saith unto them, Let us pass over unto the other side. And when they had sent away the multitude, they took him even as he was in the ship. And there were also with him other little ships. And there arose a great storm of wind, and the waves beat into the ship, so that it was now full. And he was in the hinder part of the ship, asleep on a pillow: and they awake him, and say unto him, Master, carest thou not that we perish? And he arose, and rebuked the wind, and said unto the sea, Peace, be still. And the wind ceased, and there was a great calm. And he said unto them, Why are ye so fearful? how is it that ye have no faith? And they feared exceedingly, and said one to another, What manner of man is this, that even the wind and the sea obey him" (Mark 4:35-41, KJV).

Notice their lack of faith in Christ in a storm was connected to their insecurities about Jesus caring for them. Fighting the good faith of faith requires that I know who I am in the LORD Jesus Christ. Now many of you may be thinking "Who am I?" Others might narrow that down to a title like, "Preacher," "Bishop," "Deacon," "Prophetess," or "Man/Woman of God." Still, others may think that identity is a profession such as a doctor, attorney, mechanic, professor, barber, architect, or even entrepreneur. That is not the closest thing to what I am referring to.

The word of God declares that we are "More than conquerors through Christ that loves us (Romans 8:27, KJV). Christ has never underestimated who He said you are. You are more than a conqueror even if your job laid you off. You're more than a conqueror even if someone you hoped to build a life with left you. You're more than a conqueror despite being brought up in the foster care system. You're more than a conqueror even if your father/mother told you that they wish they never had you. It was never up to them in the first place. God is the strength of our lives (Psalms 73:26) because Christ is our life, according to Colossians 3:4.

The issue is our feelings. It's not just women that are in their feelings; we all are. God created us with feelings. **Feelings are valid, but feelings lie to us every day. Feelings don't always reflect our Christ-given identity.** Feelings will make us think that we are less than who Christ has called us to be. Feelings wife make a godly wife think she is unattractive to a godly husband who is madly in love with her. Feelings will make a small and gifted child shy. Feelings can make a good mother question her motherhood. Feelings made the prophet Elijah wish to die. Feelings even made Jesus almost not go to Calvary. Psychologically speaking, every feeling of feeling not being good enough stems from a thought or thoughts of inferiority.

## Being Me Hurts

What do you do when most of your thoughts and feelings of self-loathing and unworthiness stem from the pain of being you that you didn't ask to be? Joseph did not ask to be gifted, but that was how God made him. Joseph did not ask to be able to dream and interpret dreams, but that was how God made him. Joseph did not ask to be the Governor of Egypt, but his gift made him. The irony is that God was not about to regret making Joseph the way he did because he was treated by his brothers the way he was.

**If God stops everything that made you regret being who you then you'll never appreciate who you are. Sometimes they have to hate you so you can learn to love yourself.** Check this out, the Bible never said that the day will come when his brothers stop hating him. You and I both know that just because someone eats at your table doesn't always mean they changed their mind about you. What it does mean, however, is that the Bible is right when it says, God will prepare a table for you in the presence of your enemies (Psalms 23:5).

> **If God stops everything that made you regret being who you then you'll never appreciate who you are. Sometimes they have to hate you so you can learn to love yourself.**

Have you ever had moments that you wish you were who they want? Ladies, have you ever compared yourself to the woman he left you for? Remember rapper, Lil Kim? She was so focused on the ways the girls, who her boyfriends cheated on her with, looked like she had a few surgeries. After years have gone by, many of us don't recognize her. She was trying to fix her looks to resemble European women. If you are reading this book Lil Kim, God wants you to know he loves you that you struggle to like.

Pastor Keion Henderson, of Lighthouse Church, once stated, "You better like yourself because you can't be nobody else but you." Please stop trying to mimic someone else. You only trying to be them because you haven't discovered the Christ in you. If you're not confident and content with the Christ in you, you'll minimize the gift or gifts in you due to the accolades you see the person you so desperately admire and sometimes secretly envy.

Joseph had to live with the pain of being him. Being Joseph got him stripped of his coat of many colors. Joseph germinated the betrayal in his life by his family. Being Joseph was the reason why he was sold into slavery. Being Joseph got him lied to by Potiphar's horny wife. Being Joseph also, on the other hand, allowed him to help someone else while he was going through pain himself (sound familiar?). Being Joseph got him out of jail. Being Joseph ultimately led him to be in the King's presence. Being Joseph also led him to be the prince of Egypt, with enough power to feed his family that stabbed him in the back.

## BEING ME NEVER STOPPED ME FROM LOVING MY HEARTBREAK

Additionally, being Joseph, becoming the prince of Egypt, moving on with his life, and getting a new start did not negate the fact that he carried his family in his heart. Have you ever been thinking about someone wondering if they are thinking about you? Have you ever been unable to eat over someone who went out to eat? Success does not stop the heart from wanting to it wants or loving who it loves.

These were his brothers, and there was not enough money in Joseph's account that could change that. By the time we reach Joseph at the height of his success, he is married with a family of his own. Nevertheless, Joseph wanted to help those who would not help him. Joseph wanted to do good to those that used him out of spite. He wanted to find his brother and reunite with all of his brothers. How could Joseph love those who hated him? Why does our heart crave the people who abandoned, neglected, physically, or emotionally abused us?

According to psychotherapist and licensed clinical social worker, Susan Anderson, it is the insecurities of abandonment that make one crave someone who is not good for them. She states in her book *The Journey from Abandonment to Healing:*

> "You keep going back because you're still not convinced that the one who's left is no good for you. You keep getting bruised, but the child inside believes that this time will be different. You're like the alcoholic who thinks the next time he drinks. He won't get drunk. You may get angry with others who try to nurture you. You may, for instance, lash out at your therapist, especially if she is encouraging you to stay away from your old partner. You may have agreed to leave the relationship behind, but the child may act out by missing sessions, switching sponsors, or changing recovery groups.

You're angry at your therapist and others because they speak against the wishes of the child. The child fears that, unless the urgent pleas are heard, its life is in peril. The child within clings to false hope to ward off feelings of isolation, banishment, and loss Without hope, you stay buried in despair, and those feelings evolve into profound grief, creating a bottomless well of tears."

Now let's go back to what she said as I weigh her thoughts against the plan God has for the life of Joseph. Here are a few things to consider about abandonment from a God perspective:

- This was more than craving a lover, wife, man, or friend. Joseph wants to do the God thing and feed his family. Even if he had insecurities, that was not the reason why he wanted people that betrayed him back in his life. He wants them back in his life because God had a plan that they nor Joseph could see at the moment. **Sometimes our purpose does not begin with connection- but rejection.**

- Joseph knew that his brothers were not good for him. He knew they wanted to destroy him despite his pleading against their evil deeds. However, Joseph trusted the goodness of God. He was at a place in his life where he could see God in the betrayal. Trust me, until we see God in our betrayals, we will never understand the strategic plans of the LORD Jesus Christ.

- Joseph never said he wanted them to change. Joseph never bases reuniting with them on their character; Joseph bases reuniting with them on Christ's character. I want to caution you that before you let people back in your life, count on Christ's character before you count on theirs. That does not mean that we tolerate disrespect or the same treatment they gave us in the past. It simply means that forgiving them is about trusting God's character and the change Christ has made in us.

- No one was able to talk Joseph out of helping his family because he had integrity. In fact, Joseph's identity was his integrity. Oftentimes, we mistake gifts and talents for identity. Gifts and talents are what you do, but integrity is who you are. Nobody should have to keep talking us into being who Christ has called us to be and it should be more difficult for Satan and his demons to talk us out of who Christ called us to be.

## A LESSON ON WINNING THE APPROVAL
## OF PEOPLE WHO KNOW YOUR DIRT

I digress from the life of Joseph for a moment to talk to someone reading this book that has a hard time accepting the Christ in you because of all the mistakes, sins, and consequences of their past. What happens when you have moved on with your life, but the evidence of your past is everywhere? It's on certain media sites, on their phone along with screenshots, in your criminal background checks, or even revived in the mouths of those who love to gossip. Here is what you do: You look to Jesus, hold your head up, and trust in Christ's forgiveness. It's not the first time people looked at you differently with a permanent opinion and God knows it won't be the last.

Furthermore, please stop avoiding places of judgment. Relocating doesn't stop it. Changing your phone number doesn't always make it better. Sometimes you just have to walk through the valley of the shadow of death, fearing no evil because the LORD Jesus is with you. If you don't forgive yourself (after you've asked Jesus Christ for forgiveness), you'll be a prisoner in your own mind regardless of where you go.

Additionally, what happens when someone who has the power to promote you knows your dirt? That's a real anxiety attack and faith snatcher if you think the LORD Jesus isn't on your side. What also adds insult to injury is when someone from your past, who has the information to bring you down, knows someone in your present, who has the power to bring you up. That is a lot of fear to live with. So let's cut to the chase. The Bible made it clear that promotion does come from the east or the west. It comes from the LORD (Psalms 75:6-7). Don't live in fear of your past destroying your future. **The same Jesus that is God enough to get you through your past is the same Jesus that is God enough not to let your past destroy your future.**

## "I AM JOSEPH"

"Joseph could stand it no longer. There were many people in the room, and he said to his attendants, "Out, all of you!" So he was alone with his brothers when he told them who he was. Then he broke down and wept. He wept so loudly the Egyptians could hear him, and word of it quickly carried to Pharaoh's palace. "I am Joseph!" he said to his brothers. "Is my father still alive?" But his brothers were speechless! They were stunned to realize that Joseph was standing there in front of them. "Please, come closer," he said to them. So they came closer. And he said again, "I am Joseph, your brother, whom you sold into slavery in Egypt. But don't be upset, and don't be angry with yourselves for selling me to this place. It was God who sent me here ahead of you to preserve your lives. This famine that has ravaged the land for two years will last five more years, and there will be neither plowing nor harvesting. God has sent me ahead of you to keep you and your families alive and to preserve many survivors. So it was God who sent me here, not you! And he is the one who made me an adviser to Pharaoh— the manager of his entire palace and the governor of all Egypt. "Now hurry back to my father and tell him, 'This is what your son Joseph says: God has made me master over all the land of Egypt. So come down to me immediately! You can live in the region of Goshen, where you can be near me with all *your children and grandchildren, your flocks and herds, and everything you own. I will take care of you there, for there are still five years of famine ahead of us. Otherwise you, your household, and all your animals will starve.'" Then Joseph added, "Look! You can see for yourselves, and so can my brother Benjamin, that I really am Joseph! Go tell my father of my honored position here in Egypt. Describe for him everything you have seen, and then bring my father here quickly." Weeping with joy, he embraced Benjamin, and Benjamin did the same. Then Joseph kissed each of his brothers and wept over them, and after that, they began talking freely with him"* (Genesis 45:1-13, NLT).

An ample amount of time has passed since Joseph has seen his brothers and a lot of things have changed. Joseph's status has changed. Joseph's standard of living has changed. Joseph's marital status has changed. Joseph even has children of his own. One thing, however, that did not change was his identity in God. Joseph finally reveals himself to his brothers, stating, "I am Joseph." To western culture, we see no significance in Joseph stating his name. However, in Joseph's day, a name like that carried great importance.

You see Joseph in Hebrew means, "May God add." Such an interesting meaning for a man who lost a lot in his life. He lost time with his family, the loyalty of his family, and more. Nevertheless, stripping Joseph of his coat did not stop God from adding to his life. Selling him to slavery did not decrease the freedom he had in God. Lying on him could not take the truth of God's favor in his life. Even placing him in jail could not keep God out. No wonder the meaning of Joseph's name includes God because God was the source of his identity. **Regardless of how lost you feel, you can be found if you look for your identity in the LORD Jesus Christ alone.** The fight of Joseph's life is to know who we are. Just an inch of low self-esteem is enough to make us anxious, depressed, suicidal, self-sabotaging, and over or underachievers. Sometimes it's not just what we went through in life that hurts; it's the damage it does to our sense of worth.

> **Regardless of how lost you feel, you can be found if you look for your identity in the LORD Jesus Christ alone.**

## BEFORE YOU CONFRONT THEM...

I don't know if Joseph thought in his mind what would he say to his brothers if he had a chance to see them again. Maybe he was learning to live with them. Let me pause and tell someone that is currently living with someone you ignore and give the silent treatment to. That is psychologically speaking, emotional torture, and you are teaching them how to live without you emotionally while they stay with you physically.

Let me testify on the behalf of those of us who were ready at one point to tell off the people we could not wait or are still waiting to confront. I've learned that confronting any betrayal in our lives requires having a praying life, Christ-confidence, and a resolve to confront the problem and not the person. There are only two ways to confront those who hurt you. One we can confront them to get them to know who we are out of our insecurities. Or we can confront them because we know who we are out of a Christ-Confidence. The speech Joseph gave his brother gives us some guidelines on confronting those who hurt us.

1. **Know that they cannot give you YOU**. What do I mean by this? Joseph was related to them, and had their blood, but was in a class all by himself. He had the favor of God in his life, and there was absolutely nothing that his brothers' evil plot could do to them. Joseph is no longer looking for them to be like him. In fact, he forgives them for who they are not. Until we can forgive people for who they are not, we will always be bitter over who they are and who have been to us.

2. **Confront them without waiting on them to be accountable**. Everyone we confront will not own up to it. Notice you read nowhere they took responsibility after Joseph reveals himself to them. Sometimes, the confrontation isn't about making them accountable but letting them know you're not going to lose sleep if they don't.

3. **You may have to give them the closure you were looking for.** Notice Joseph tells them not to be angry with themselves. Wow! It takes a Christ-Confident individual to say that. He is not asking why. He has no more questions about what they did.

4. **"Is My Father alive?".** Now that was Joseph's only question to them in the above passage. I don't know what you have gone through, and who left you for dead, your Father is alive and well! I am talking about

the almighty God. As long as He lives, your dream can never die, and I am a living witness.

5. **Be prepared to help them again.** Now I have to admit, this one was even a struggle for me (Laugh out Loud). Often we pride ourselves on everything we have accomplished without the assistance of those who left us along the way or refused to help us. However, everything we have came from the LORD Jesus. Don't you ever forget that. We used to sing an old song growing up in my grandmother's church, "You can't beat God no matter how you try, the more you give, the more he gives to you. Just keep on giving because it's true. You can't beat God's giving. No matter how hard you try."

## "Joseph is Still Alive"

That's what his brothers told their father, Jacob when they returned home. Now the scripture makes it clear that they did not tell the whole story, but one thing for certain is that their plan did not work. I want you to pause and lift your hands toward heaven, thanking the LORD Jesus that you didn't just survive; you overcame what your insecurities make you think would destroy you. What you overcame proves that in the LORD Jesus Christ, you are an overcomer!

## What if Joseph turns into us?

Now let me speak on behalf of Joseph's brothers for a minute. Only low self-worth could birth the magnitude of hate and jealousy that would make them even think about letting him die in that pit. What they did was not right but what they did disclosed how they saw themselves. One thing I can say for sure is that I have learned over the years to look at how people treat us which does not add up. Let's take this a step further: **Sometimes, forgiving your enemies means understanding you're forgiving them for not loving themselves.**

> **Sometimes, forgiving your enemies means understanding you're forgiving them for not loving themselves.**

They might have been waiting for Joseph to turn into them and give them the same treatment that they have him in the past. Now that is a special kind of paranoia. Sometimes the people who hurt us never planned on needing or running to us again, Nevertheless, always keep in mind that it is a strong possibility that we will run into people who hurt us or even people we have hurt in the past. If we were in the wrong, repent, forgive yourself, and ask for their forgiveness. How- ever, remember that not everyone is going to forgive us, and that is ok. Their lack of acceptance of your apology doesn't stop God from accepting your confession and repentance to him. Or if you are the one who was treated unjustly, remember that God is always up to something good even if he has to use the people who hurt us to bless us.

## THE ANATOMY OF ME

Temptation cannot lure us in until it makes us think we are less than who the LORD Jesus Christ called us to be. Now let's not forget that we have already pointed out in previous chapters that the Bible says:

> *"Let no man say when he is tempted, I am tempted of God: for God cannot be tempted with evil, neither tempteth he any man: But every man is tempted, when he is drawn away of his own lust, and enticed. Then when lust hath conceived, it bringeth forth sin: and sin, when it is finished, bringeth forth death. Do not err, my beloved brethren"* *(James 1:13-16).*

There are some noteworthy things about the above passage. One, God is not tempting us to be what He has not called us to be. We are his beloved. However, it is our own lust that wants to pull us away from our walk with and in Christ. Our own lust comes from our insecurities and self-doubt. Lastly, who the LORD Jesus Christ has called us to be will bring life and that is everlasting life. James tells us not to make errors, which means we have the power of the Holy Spirit to keep us from falling.

Additionally, I want to take you to a spiritual anatomy class for a moment and remind you of why you should be confident in Christ even in the face of your many temptations:

- **The Mind**- the Bible makes it clear that it is with the mind that we serve the LORD (Romans 7:25). The greatest commandment is that we love the LORD our God with all our mind (Mark 12:30). The battleground for spiritual warfare has always been and will be our mind. **The reason why Satan is after**

**our minds is because he knows the truth that he cannot change Christ's mind about us.** While we go back and forth in our head, wondering if we are worth it or not, Satan is fighting us mentally making us think it's our internal dialogue. That is why we have to rehearse the word of God in our minds and be filled with the Holy Ghost. It is the Holy Spirit that will remind of us God's word in those moments of temptation

> The reason why Satan is after our minds is because he knows the truth that he cannot change Christ's mind about us.

- **Our Ears-** Many of us cannot embrace who we are in Christ because of the plethora of negative things that we have heard over the years about ourselves. In the case of Joseph's brothers, they nicknamed him "the dreamer," and asked rhetorical questions to make him feel the same insecurities that they were feeling. Sometimes the only way to recover from negative words or the words we wished we would have heard is to hear the word of God. The Bible teaches that faith comes by hearing the word of God (Romans 10:17). Trust and believe that I know for myself that there was positively no way that I could have overcome the words of those close to me without the word of God.

- **Our Heart-** The interesting thing about the heart is that the Bible calls it "deceitful" (Jeremiah 17:9). Now come on, who wants to hear that their heart - not could be, but is deceitful? I know I don't, but it's vital to know. Our hearts are the seat of our emotions. Our hearts will make us think that we want people that we don't want. We could just be heartbroken at the moment. Our hearts can get us locked behind bars, waste time on people that Christ never wanted us in the first place, and sabotage our journey. The heart can only be trusted when the word of God is in it: *"Thy word have I hid in my heart that I might not sin against thee" (Psalms 119:11).*

- **Our Eyes**- During the moment of temptation our identity in Christ Jesus the LORD looks smaller in comparison to what we are craving. For temptation to look big, we have to feel small without the thing, person or place that the flesh is craving. Here me when I tell you that you don't need what or who you think you need to feel good about yourself. The Bible teaches us to look to Jesus (Hebrews 12:2) because He is the author and finisher of our faith. The temptation will only end in death. Whether it is the death of our health due to many sexual partners, the death of our wealth on supporting our substance use problem, the death of our marriage, or the death of meaningful relationships with the people that God has placed in our lives.

- **Our Hands and Feet**- Oh yes! We have to watch what we put our hands on and where we take our feet. Some things can contaminate us more than we can clean them. There are places where many have gone in and lost their lives. That brother enjoyed sleeping with that married woman in her husband's bed until the husband walked in and caught them. Be careful what internet place your hands on because your feet will want to take a trip there. Keep your feet on solid ground while knowing Jesus Christ is the solid rock.

## What Does the Temptation to Wish I was Someone Else Have to do with My Destiny?

Do you realize how high many gifted individuals could have soared if they had discovered their true identity in the LORD Jesus Christ, who is the Almighty God? Do you realize how much of the sins we have committed and backsliding we have done had the seeds of inferiority planted in them? Some of us, despite how much the LORD Jesus Christ has afforded us to win on the level He placed us on, are still comparing ourselves to others who have millions of followers on social media and seem to surpass us in life.

Hear me, we can never be who we are jealous of. That is what Joseph's brothers even understand. Since that could not be them, they wanted to kill him. Joseph was uniquely designed by the mighty hand of the Most High God! Why are you ruining your vocal cords trying to be a soprano when the LORD Jesus Christ has gifted you to be a tenor like no other? Why are you trying to preach like someone else whose gift will only work for them when the style that God has given you will reach who He wants it to reach?

Part of accepting ourselves for who Christ has made us to be is accepting the fact that everyone will not accept us nor be impressed with us. Jesus Christ made the world, and the world still is not impressed with Jesus. Many doubt Him, and some just see Him as merely a good man. So the next time we say we want to be like Jesus Christ, we have to remember Jesus Christ wasn't respected, accepted, or admired by many, but that never stopped Him from being God.

You don't have to go back to drugs because you didn't get the job bro. You don't have to sell your body to put yourself through school, my sister. You don't have to binge eat to look like the models in the magazine. I hope the degree you're pursuing is the one God has placed in your heart and not out of a need for competition with another sibling or to let your parents live their dreams through you. Who the LORD Jesus Christ has called us to be will always, always, and I mean always be enough. Why? Because Jesus Christ is enough. So tell your temptations that "Jesus can satisfy me because Jesus Christ is God."

# "But God is faithful..."

*"The temptations in your life are no different from what others experience. And God is faithful. He will not allow the temptation to be more than you can stand. When you are tempted, he will show you a way out so that you can endure"* (1 Corinthians 10:13, NLT).

Sometimes I wondered why didn't Joseph commit suicide. After reading about his life, that was enough to send anyone into a state of depression. Then I reminded myself that Joseph was not the first person betrayed, and he definitely won't be the last. Every temptation that ever came across his path only confirmed the fact that his destiny was still going to happen. That is what the LORD Jesus Christ wants you to know that your destiny is still going to happen. Your destiny is bigger than what you had in mind. Your destiny is God's will for your life. Joseph was in the will of God.

Remember, Satan was not mentioned anywhere in Joseph's story. What we do see, however, is that the favor of God never left him. I use to think that being a dreamer and having the gift to interpret dreams was pretty cool for Joseph. However, if we relegate Joseph's success to his dreams, we have missed the lesson in the blessing of the climax of his story. A significant part of Joseph's life is that the Bible kept saying that "The LORD was with Joseph" (Genesis 39:2-3,21).

Now did it look like God was with him? No. However, we see in retrospect that there is no way this brother could have survived that level of betrayal by family, false allegations by the seducing married woman, and imprisonment for saying "no" to fornication if God was not with this brother. Why did God place him in that family? The real question is how could he be in that kind of family if God didn't have a purpose and destiny for him to fulfill. The question is not why didn't God clear his name when Potiphar's wife lied on him. The real question is how could Joseph resist if he didn't have trust and confidence in his God.

Moreover, how could Joseph deny the temptation to not get even when God placed him in a position of power? Joseph endured that what God does not take away, He gives us the power to endure. That is why the Bible makes it clear that we are blessed if we endure the temptation that is meant to bring us down, embarrass us, lock us up, and destroy our marriage, ministry, or even our health.

Some of you may be saying, "Curtis I hear you, but I read this book too late. I already messed up. I lost my wife." "I have HIV." "My career is ruined." "God doesn't love nobody like me." You still think you read this by accident. Even if you didn't pray before you went down, or prayed and took God for granted, you could not out-sin God's grace. If you're a backslider, come back home. All God wants you to do is repent. If you never committed your life to the LORD Jesus Christ, all you have to do is, *"Repent and be baptized every one of you in the name of Jesus*

*Christ for the remission of your sins, and you shall receive the gift of the holy ghost"* (Acts 2:38, NKJV).

On the other hand, others may be saying, "No I'm already saved. I'm just worried about falling again." Hear me, if Jesus is God enough to pick you up out of a life of sin, guilt, and shame, he is certainly God enough to keep you from falling now. In fact, the Bible says, *"Now unto him (Jesus Christ) that is able to keep you from falling and to present you faultless before the presence of his glory with exceeding joy"* (Jude 1:24, KJV). Yes, not only can Christ keep us from falling, he can restore our joy, removing the guilt and shame like it never happens.

Temptations do not go away. However, the Holy Spirit is there to strengthen us and guide us into all truth. The Bible never said there was any sin in being tempted. Don't forget, even the LORD Jesus Christ was tempted. The sin is in yielding (and Jesus never sinned nor could He because there was no sin in Him). So how did Christ face temptations? The answer is with the word of God. Jesus did not just have a word; He is the word. When the word of God is our defense in the face of temptation, we can agree with Joseph when he told his brothers what that means for evil, God made it good (Genesis 50:20).

So you see because we know that all things work together for the good of them who love God, who are called according to his purpose (Romans 8:28). We can certainly say that it's all good. Even the things that broke our hearts, traumatized us, or even made us choose to go down the wrong path did not stop God from loving us. We see that God was still and is good to us despite what happened to us and the decisions we regret making or had to make along the way to survive. My prayer for you and me is that we will not be led into temptation. However, if we are, the next prayer is that we will be delivered from evil in Jesus' NAME.